A GOOD LITTLE GALLIMAUFRY

A miscellany of writing linked to Essex

Edited by

Patrick Forsyth & Lloyd Bonson

This Edition Published by Stanhope Books, Essex, UK 2016

www.stanhopebooks.com

Cover design and format by Susan Hilton and Lloyd Bonson © 2016

We are grateful to be able to reproduce the cover image from one of the beautiful glass
windows in Farleigh's Sanctuary designed by Susan Hilton.

ISBN-13: 978-1-909893-08-5

PREFACE

Essex is a diverse county with much within its bounds ranging from cities and industrial areas to quaint market towns, rural countryside and villages and a long and varied coastline.

All the writers whose work is presented here live in or have close connections with Essex, or have such a link within their writing here.

All the writers in this work have contributed without financial reward, but have the satisfaction of knowing **that the royalty element from the book's sales will go to help the patients and family who use the services of Farleigh Hospice.**

As a Trustee of Essex's Farleigh Hospice – and a writer myself – I am pleased to have been involved in the assembling and publication of this book and am grateful to Lloyd Bonson of Stanhope Books for his support of the project. The reputation of Farleigh is well known, their services, most supplied out in the community rather than at their centre near Broomfield hospital, are exemplary (and I know this from personal experience). Their continuing operation is dependent in large part on voluntary donations ranging from a few coins in their collection boxes to purchases in their shops and legacies in wills. More details of Farleigh's activities (and how you can help it) appear at the end of this book.

So let me address a huge thank you all those who have made this book possible, to those who wrote for it, published it and publicise it and, of course, those readers who have bought copies. Anything and everything that helps support the activities of Farleigh is worthwhile; in this case the book will perhaps act as a more permanent reminder of their good work.

Finally, there is some good reading ahead. Enjoy.

Patrick Forsyth
Trustee: Farleigh Hospice.

CONTENTS

PATRICK FORSYTH lives in Maldon. Well known as a writer of business material (for instance *Effective Time Management* [Kogan Page]), he has more recently turned his hand to other things. He has had a humorous book published, three books of travel writing, including *First class – at last!* contrasting budget and first class travel during a journey on the Eastern & Oriental train running from Singapore through Malaysia to Thailand, and most recently a novel, *Long Overdue,* also published by Stanhope Books. An earlier version of the following story won second prize in a national short story competition run by the prestigious Society of Women Writers & Journalists. He writes regularly for "Writing Magazine" and can be contacted via: www.patrickforsyth.com

BRUSHING AWAY THE PAST

He moved forward slowly and steadily, his eyes scanning from side to side as he planted his feet carefully amidst the rubble, which shifted disconcertingly as he moved. The earthquake had occurred only hours ago doing substantial damage to the nearby village. Around him scores of people, clad in florescent jackets like his and wearing yellow hard hats moved around the buildings near him, rescue vehicles threaded their way amongst the rubble and sirens wailed in the background. On several wrecked houses flames were being doused and smoke rose through the dusty air. "Listen up." George called out and began to get things organised.

All around buildings were in different states of collapse: some virtually untouched, others worse than the building he moved across. He climbed over a long concrete beam, and saw that the specially trained dog that preceded him had stopped and was nosing into a crevice. Its tail raised high and wagging, it seemed to have found something - or rather someone - and given his dog's training that meant someone was still alive.

George caught up with the dog, moved his feet into what seemed stable positions and crouched down. He looked around him and called out.

"Quiet everyone." Then he shouted into the crevice.

"Is anyone there? Can you hear me?"

Always such moments could be heart-stopping, when a sound was heard amongst the devastation indicating the chance of a survivor and the possibility that a life might be saved. He stooped lower, listening. Presently he heard a faint reply.

"Hello. Help me - please help me." The voice was clearly female.

"Help's coming, how are you doing?" He called back, adding quickly "What's your name?" It was Jenny.

"I'm okay, but it's dark. I can't move."

"Is anyone else there?" Whatever else he might have wanted to say he had to get the facts straight.

"Only Billy." Jenny's voice sounded distant, but though weak it was clear and audible.

"Is Billy alright?"

There was silence for a moment … then: "He says he is, but he's got cobwebs on his face and he hates spiders."

George added reassurance, insisting it was probably just dust, he repeated that help was near.

"We'll have you out of there soon," he said. "Just let me tell people where you are."

He stood up carefully. Although Jenny was apparently not too deeply buried, lifting equipment would be necessary, and, on George's instructions, within minutes other men had gathered around and a crane was positioned carefully.

"Hello Jenny, we're digging now," he called again down into the rubble. "Are you still alright?"

The voice was still faint. "Yes, I think so, and Billy says we'll be okay."

"How're you doing Billy?" he called.

Again there was a long pause before Jenny replied, "He says we're fine."

"Can he shout to me?"

Another pause. "No, he doesn't want to talk."

George wondered if that meant Billy was in some way injured, but just said,

"Okay, not long now."

The rubble around was gently being moved, carefully so as not to precipitate any further collapse. A large concrete beam was unearthed and the crane was able to lift that clear making further digging easier.

"Nearly there," he called.

There was no reply. He called again, moments later the voice answered, but it was weaker now.

"Please hurry, Billy's wants to get out."

Caught up in all that it was necessary to do George had only thought of the person as a live one to be saved, now listening to the weak little voice he realised how young Jenny sounded.

"How old are you?" He called. Again a pause.

"I'm five and a half, but Billy's older, he's looking after me."

"That's good - how old's Billy then?"

He attempted to keep the conversation going and wanted to ask about parents and perhaps begin taking steps to reunite the family. If Jenny's parents were alive somewhere they would be distraught, wondering where the kids were and if they had survived. But that would come later. He called again, but this time there was no reply.

He called and called but neither Jenny nor Billy answered. Nothing further was heard as the careful digging continued and a little over an hour later they reached the body of the little girl. She lay curled up face down, protected under a heavy wooden table, but her leg had received a gash and she had bled to death. Her face was coated in the dust she had feared was cobwebs. She was one of dozens of people killed, but to George she was special. He would remember her quavering voice until his dying day.

"And she thought she was almost out." George spoke out loud to no one in particular, thinking that she had probably had no intimation of what was happening.

But what about Billy? George could see now that Jenny was alone, but when they gently lifted out her little body, there, clutched in her arms, was a teddy bear, rather old by the look of it and with one eye conspicuously askew. The bear was ingrained in dust, but George could see it wore a sky-blue t-shirt with the word "Billy" on it. Later George would pass it on to those collecting the various personal effects unearthed as the rescue crew worked on; now a shout and a barking dog pulled his attention elsewhere.

*

A year later and many thousands of miles distant Mary drove a battered open-topped Land Rover across the African bush. The word Oxfam was emblazoned on its side. Dressed in khaki with a hat to protect her from the heat her wheels threw up red dust, which rose in her wake as she headed for the orphanage located in a small village twenty miles from her current base. An Oxfam volunteer, she was part of a team installing fresh water supplies around villages in the area, but this monthly delivery to the orphanage was her own private project, she brought whatever little extras she could to help the children – all of whom had been rescued from difficult pasts, but who were now safe and getting closer to normality.

The hot sun burnt down and she arrived at the cluster of tin roofed buildings in late morning ready for a break and a refreshing drink. She parked outside the main residence and in the shade of a tree, but was only half out of the vehicle before she was surrounded by a crowd of bright eyed children laughing and cheering. They knew Mary's visits meant presents and their excitement was palpable. Deciding to put her drink on hold, Mary called out cheery hellos, moved to the back of the Land Rover and began to unload battered, much-used cardboard boxes. These contained everything from clothes to kitchen utensils and brightly coloured mugs. But one box was special, containing toys she had collected from various well-wishers.

"You can all have something from here," she said "Just one thing each mind. Make sure everyone gets something."

Smiling and laughing the children fell on the box like starving jackals and each ran off with something: simple things: a spinning top, a kite, a jigsaw puzzle and more. Little Nelson, clad in bleached denim shorts and a faded red t-shirt was last to approach the box. He had been found abandoned and badly beaten before being taken in by the orphanage and still walked with a limp, one bare foot dragging a little behind the other; though he was improving every day he could not yet cope with the scrum around the box. But one toy was left.

"What have you got?" Mary asked, worried that his being last might have short-changed him.

"A teddy bear Miss," he said, adding: "Thank you."

He smiled shyly. The bear looked a bit battered and sported a t-shirt indicating that its name was Billy.

"He's called Billy," said Mary pointing out the letters to Nelson, who at six was just starting to read.

Nelson studied the bear intently in the way only a six year old can do, he turned it slowly from side to side and then clutched it firmly to his chest. But a moment later he pulled it away from himself and shook it. Mary lent forward and brushed the bear's face.

"It's just dust," she said. "He's a little battered, but I'll help you clean him up later."

Nelson turned the bear so that they were face to face just a few inches apart. He knew nothing of Billy's history, of course, not his trauma of a year ago or how he had spent the subsequent months in darkness - in boxes that had ultimately crossed the world.

"He's fine," he said. "But ... he does have a rather a sad face. I'll cheer him up - I'm sure we will soon be special friends. We'll look after each other forever."

Mary smiled and imagined that Billy looked as if he might agree wholeheartedly with Nelson's comments. Indeed maybe he would say so later ... when he and Nelson had got to know each other a little better.

Footnote

Farleigh Hospice is dependent in large part not on any official funding, but on donations. One way money is raised is through its fourteen shops. Donations of many sorts are made and some items so given to charity shops may be passed on more than once; as may be the case here. Imagine: it could all have started in Maldon.

Sheila Norton was born, and went to school, in Romford, and now lives in Galleywood. Most of her working life was spent as a medical secretary. Having worked at St Andrew's Hospital in Billericay, she moved with the rest of the staff to Broomfield Hospital in 1998. Sheila has been writing for most of her life, having had her first novel published in 2003 after serving a long apprenticeship with short stories. She is now retired from the day job and is working on her fifteenth novel.

For more information: www.sheilanorton.com

THE LAMP

"We've got enough souvenirs now, Lisa. Let's go, or we'll be late for the airport transfer."

Lisa looked at her watch and shook her head.

"We've got ages yet. And I just wanted to have another look at this little lamp. I'd really like it, Gary – I think it's lovely."

"Lovely? He wants three hundred dirhams for it! Honestly, Lise …"

"That's only about thirty pounds – and I'll barter him down, anyway," Lisa hissed back, as the trader smiled at them and held up the lamp for their closer inspection.

Gary was being so mean, she thought irritably. They'd walked round the souk twice and all he'd agreed to buy was a cheap necklace for his own mum and a leather wallet for himself. This long weekend in Marrakech was supposed to be a make-or-break holiday for them, a chance for them to be away on their own together to talk through their differences and hopefully restore a bit of the romance that seemed to have gone out of their relationship recently. Instead, they'd bickered more than ever.

She held out her hand for the pretty little lamp as the trader passed it to her. There were lots of similar objects on the stalls here – ironwork candleholders designed to stand on a table or shelf, or to hang outside on a patio – but his one was different from all the others she'd seen.

"This one is very old, very *ancient*," said the trader, showing off his excellent tourism English. "It has come from a Berber family living high in the Atlas Mountains. It was in their family from father to son, father to son, for – how do you say it? – many *generations*."

"Believe that, and you'll believe anything," muttered Gary at Lisa's elbow, but Lisa refused to listen. Whether the story was true or not, she felt it made the lamp seem just that little bit more special.

"Also, it is for good luck," went on the trader, his eyes sparkling with the anticipation of a sale. "Put it in your house, and it will keep away all sadness."

"Yeah, right!" Gary exclaimed out loud, turning away and beginning to walk off.

Lisa stared after him. He obviously expected her to follow him, but she really wanted to buy this lamp. She knew the little story was nonsense but it was a bit of fun, and she wanted something for herself, something to take back with her from Marrakech other than the sad, sinking feeling that her marriage was falling apart.

"I'll give you one hundred dirhams for it," she offered the trader.

"Sorry. Not enough," he replied, still smiling. "Two hundred and fifty I would accept."

"No. Two hundred, then."

"Madam, you will make me a poor man." He laughed and wrapped the lamp for her. "Here – I will accept two hundred dirhams, just for you, because you are a beautiful lady and you look so sad. I hope it will bring you happiness."

"Thank you." As Lisa got out her purse and paid him, she wondered whether it was really so obvious that she was unhappy.

***

A few weeks previously, in a village high in the Atlas Mountains, Hafeza had been looking speculatively at the old lamp that had stood for years on the shelf at the back of her family's living quarters. She couldn't remember it ever being used, but Mother- in-Law said it had been in the family for ever. She picked it up, turned it over in her hands and wondered if it was worth much. Probably not – she'd heard from the traders who sometimes came this way, taking goods from the co-operatives to the markets in Marrakech, that such things were two-a-penny on the tourist stalls.

She put it back, sighing, and went on with sweeping the floors.

"Leave the lamp alone, Hafeza," snapped Mother-in-Law, who'd been watching her from her mattress on the bedroom floor. "I keep telling you, I'm not letting you sell it! It keeps the bad things from happening to this house – you understand?"

"So why do they happen anyway?" Hafeza retorted. "Why, if your stupid lamp is so lucky, are you so crippled with arthritis that you can't stand up any more? Why did our two lambs die this year and why did our cow stop producing any milk? Why does my son have to leave school when he's twelve next month, and work in the fields instead of going to the secondary school in the city?"

"Not this again!" said Mother-in-Law impatiently. "All the kids around here finish school at twelve, you know that. This isn't Marrakech, where you grew up, with your spoilt, rich, city ways. None of the families around here can afford to send their kids to secondary school. Get used to it! And get on with your work, woman!"

Tears stinging her eyes, Hafeza picked up the broom again. She didn't want her lovely, gentle husband to come home to find her fighting with his domineering mother yet again. She knew he was worried enough about how the family were going to survive this year, without hearing her whingeing again about Saïd's education. But it was so unfair!

His teacher had told them what a bright boy Saïd was, how seriously they needed to consider sending him to secondary school so that he could fulfil his potential. Hafeza's parents in Marrakech would gladly have the boy staying with them during term time, would feed and clothe him and even help with school expenses. But the family here needed him to work in the fields, and Mother-in-Law was furious at the suggestion of accepting *charity* from Hafeza's 'rich' father. In fact he was a humble chef, but he worked hard for a good employer, a Frenchman running a small hotel in Marrakech.

"I will not allow my family to be beholden to foreigners!" screamed Mother-in-Law from her mattress. "And don't even *think* of mentioning your disgraceful *tourism* idea."

Far from being disgraceful, Hafeza knew that her idea could actually save this family from destitution. She also knew that privately, her husband agreed with her. They'd talked it over many times, in whispers when Mother-in-Law was asleep.

"Salima's family, in the next village, started doing it six months ago," she'd told him. "Salima says they were nervous at first: it felt odd to open their doors to complete strangers – Europeans and Americans who don't understand Moroccan ways and who would stare at everything and take photos of their rooms, their animals beneath the house, and so on. But once they became more accustomed to it, they found that the tourists were polite, friendly and grateful to be shown our traditions, to be treated as guests in their house and given mint tea and traditional bread – now they are happy about it. Even Salima's mother-in-law is happy!"

"But *my* mother would *never* be happy with it," her husband had replied gloomily.

Hafeza bit back the retort that his mother would never be happy with anything – least of all her son's choice of wife.

"It's a pity," was all she said instead. "We would only have to host one or two groups of tourists, and we'd quickly make up for the loss of the lambs. If we did it often enough, we could pay for Saïd to go to the secondary school."

She watched her husband struggling with his thoughts. She knew it wasn't fair to push him – his loyalties were divided. But she knew he wanted a chance for his son, as much as she did.

Later that night, when Mother-in-Law was asleep, Hafeza took the lamp down from the shelf again and blew the dust off it. It might not be very special, but it was certainly old, and she knew from her early life in Marrakech that there was no telling what tourists would pay for the most unlikely objects.

The next time the trader came into the village with his donkey cart, she smuggled the lamp out of the house under her apron and ran to meet him.

"I want to sell it," she told him, holding up the lamp. "What will you give me?"

"Huh!" He snorted with derision. "I've told you before, Hafeza. Such things are commonplace in the souks. I don't want it. I'd never get rid of it."

"Please. It's very old; it's been in my husband's family for ever. And there's a story," she added desperately, "that it brings good luck. Gets rid of sadness from people's lives, or whatever."

"Huh!" He said again. But he glanced at Hafeza and his face softened. He'd known her since she was a young girl in Marrakech, sitting on the steps of her father's kitchen at the hotel. They'd actually been at school together and he'd been sorry when she got married off to this poor farmer in the mountains. He'd never been able to understand it – he was sure she deserved a better match; someone such as himself – but according to gossip around the souk, Hafeza's father had owed this poor family a favour. Something that went back generations. And the gossip now was that Hafeza's father wanted to help with the grandson's education, too, but that evil old mother-in-law was blocking it for some reason.

"Give it here, then," he said, more roughly than he meant, to hide his sympathy. "I'll give you fifty dirhams for it."

"What!" She thrust the lamp behind her back. "Never! It's worth far more than that!"

"Look, Hafeza, I want to help, but I'm not bankrupting myself over it. A hundred dirhams, then – and that's final. It'll turn to rust before I sell it, you know."

"You were my school friend, but you're robbing me blind," she told him half-affectionately, having actually no idea whatever of the lamp's value. "Take it, then – and if it makes you a fortune, you owe me."

"Done." He shook her hand and paid her, and watched as she slid the money out of sight into her apron pocket. "Don't tell the old witch," he added grimly as he rode away.

But there was never any need to tell Mother-in-Law, as it happened. That same morning, without even waking from sleep, she passed quietly away to a far more gentle death than many people might have felt she deserved. She was over eighty and had upset half the village during her lifetime. Even her own son's tears were soon drying after the funeral – he'd loved her with filial duty but never felt much affection or loyalty in return.

"I will run this family now, the way I wish," he told Hafeza solemnly the following week. "And my first wish is for you to speak to the tourism people about hosting groups of tourists. My son *will* go to school; he will become a clever man who doesn't have to work in the fields. Perhaps a doctor, who will help poor old people like my mother and prevent them becoming crippled with pain."

He didn't notice the missing lamp. Hafeza put the money towards buying the necessary school uniform for her son. The rest was provided by the tourists who came every week in a small group to enjoy her mint tea and traditional bread. And also with the help of Hafeza's father, whose debt of gratitude to the poor village where his own father had been raised as an orphan could never be entirely repaid.

The next time the trader came to the village, Hafeza was surprised and pleased to hear that the lamp had been sold very quickly.

"I didn't make any profit," the trader told her rather untruthfully. "But I was glad to get rid of it. The tourists fell for that silly good luck story."

Hafeza had been thinking about that story. Of course, she knew it was nonsense; the lamp certainly hadn't brought any luck when it was in her house. And as soon as she'd sold it, her life had improved immeasurably. So much for silly old superstitions!

***

Lisa had put the lamp on a table in her lounge. Of course, it didn't stay there for long as it was only a matter of weeks before she and Gary were separating all their belongings and preparing to sell the house.

"It's beautiful," her sister said, when she came to help Lisa pack her things. She was moving into a tiny one-bedroomed flat while Gary stayed in the house until it was sold. She knew it wasn't fair; everyone had told her it wasn't fair, but she was so tired of all the arguments with Gary, she'd just given in, and would probably give in to all his unfair demands, just as long as he'd agree to the divorce.

"You can keep it, if you like," she said sadly. "It won't look right in the flat. Anyway, it was supposed to bring good luck, according to the guy who sold it to me. So much for that!"

"Ah, Lisa – I'll look after it for you if you like, until all this is sorted out, but you know, I'm sure everything will work out for you eventually," said her sister kindly, giving her a hug. She turned the lamp over in her hands. "What does the inscription on the bottom mean?"

"Inscription?" Lisa frowned as she looked at it. "I didn't even realise there was an inscription. I thought it was part of the pattern."

"I think it's Arabic. Wouldn't it be nice to know what it says?"

"I suppose so." Lisa smiled at her sister. "I'll leave that to you."

Her sister took the lamp to a friend whose cousin's neighbour's son in the next street had studied ancient Arabic. When the son of the neighbour finally got to see the lamp, he studied the inscription very carefully and eventually wrote down the translation, which he passed to his father, who then passed it to his neighbour, who eventually remembered to bring the lamp back to her cousin, Lisa's sister's friend, who finally turned up with it on a Saturday when Lisa and her sister were sitting together in Lisa's tiny rented flat.

The friend handed the translation to Lisa's sister and they invited her to join them for a glass of wine.

"Apparently," said Lisa's sister, "it means: *Happiness fills the house if the lamp is lit. Sadness fills the house when the lamp is cold. Death or divorce will occur if the lamp is sold; but happiness will follow.*"

"Oh – my – God!" Lisa said, looking at her sister and beginning to laugh. "How funny is that?"

"We're just having a drink to celebrate Lisa's divorce," her sister explained. "She's very happy about it – especially as her ex has just, unexpectedly agreed to give in and settle the financial stuff amicably – and a lot more generously than we ever thought he would!"

"That's great!" agreed the friend. "So what's funny about this inscription?"

"He hated the lamp," Lisa laughed. "But I'm glad I bought it! It was the turning point, really – he was so mean about it, it made me realise how much he'd changed, and how little we had left in common."

"I'm only looking after it for you, remember. You can have it back when you move again," her sister reminded Lisa, running her fingers over the inscription. "I don't believe any of this stuff – of course! – but it's a nice thought, that it might have brought you some happiness. You'd better light a candle in it, Lise – keep it alight! I wonder what its story was, back in Morocco – who sold it … and whether it brought them good or bad luck."

"Who knows? It's all just superstition really, isn't it," said Lisa.

***

On that same day, in a mud-hut village, high in the Atlas mountains of Morocco, a twelve-year-old boy was proudly wearing his new uniform and preparing to leave his parents' home for the long journey to the school in Marrakech.

"I sold the lamp," his mother finally admitted to her husband as they watched the child climb into the donkey-cart. "I sold the old family lamp, out of desperation to see this dream come true. It was the day your mother died. I forgot to tell you."

"It doesn't matter," said her husband. "I would have sold my mother, if I could, to make this happen." He gave her a hug as he added, thoughtfully, "I never really liked that lamp. It had some ancient writing on the bottom of it, that neither Mother nor I could understand. I don't know why she was so determined never to sell it."

"I'm glad I got rid of it, then," Hafeza said. "Nobody ever lit it, anyway."

Amanda Brandon was born and raised in Essex. She won a story writing competition at the age of 13 which inspired her to forge a writing career.

She worked as a journalist for a leading county newspaper for 13 years before turning to writing fiction when her children started school.

Her first book for children *A Scarf and a Half* about knitting loving Granny Mutton and grandson Little Lionel was chosen for the Reading Agency's 2015 summer reading challenge. Her second book, *A Box of Socks* was published earlier the same year and she is currently working on the third book in the series due out in 2016.

The books have helped her bring farmyard fun to book festivals and schools in Essex and Suffolk and in 2014 she co-wrote a local history church centenary book.

For more details of Amanda's work go to www.amandabrandon.co.uk

A Taste For Murder

A grey-haired woman slumped in the corner of the store cupboard. Brown cake crumbs scattered her apron. Her head lolled to one side and rested on a shelf of cinnamon brownies.

Callie clutched the door frame and leaned forward. "Yes, that's Joyce, my shop assistant." The police officer put a guiding hand under her elbow and led her away. It was clear that Joyce's baking days were over and Callie's Cake Shop would be closed until further notice.

Callie suspected Joyce had been stealing from the store cupboard but she didn't mention it to the police. "It only makes matters worse," she told members of her baking circle later.

"The police said it was an unfortunate accident. She tripped and caught her head on the heavy wooden shelf. The door clicked shut and trapped her inside. By the time I found her it was too late."

Helen helped herself to another cinnamon swirl. The death of her neighbour hadn't dampened her appetite. "Who would have thought it, Joyce caught with her hands in the cookie jar or rather the cake cupboard."

The rest of Callie's baking circle shook their heads.

"There was something a bit too high and mighty about Miss Joyce. She thought she was better than us, particularly after she started work here."

"Really Helen, you shouldn't speak ill of the dead." Mary tutted. Her cake was untouched on her plate. She didn't feel like eating.

It was true Callie thought, Joyce had given off an air of superiority, although she had good reason. Whether anyone had liked her or not her cakes were always superbly presented and beautifully iced. Callie taught cake baking and decorating to a small group of enthusiasts on a Wednesday evening. Joyce had been the most skilled and Callie offered her a job in the shop. Joyce had proved useful if a touch too keen.

Helen ignored Mary's disapproval. "I thought you of all people wouldn't want to defend her. She always criticised your efforts."

Mary sniffed. "It was unkind, but I just ignored her digs. I know I'm not the greatest baker in the world."

She added, "Callie's a great teacher and I enjoy carving sugar flowers and designing delicate decorations, it's relaxing. I'll admit I was envious of Joyce's cakes. She created such dainty flowers but I wouldn't want to see the poor woman dead."

Mary knew Helen rarely found a good word to say about Joyce. The two had fallen out after she bought a terrier which barked non-stop according to Helen.

"All this talk of death makes me queasy," Tina said. She was the newest member of the baking circle. Recently divorced she had joined after losing her job. Her doctor had advised her to take up a new hobby. She'd always enjoyed making cakes and when she saw Callie's advert she thought she'd give it a go.

"May I have a glass of water, Callie?" She looked at her hostess apologetically.

"Yes of course," Callie rose from the table, grateful for the diversion. "I'll get everyone a drink. Could you give me a hand?"

Tina followed her into the kitchen. "To think Joyce was stuck in the store cupboard all night. It's terrible. I hate confined spaces. What a tragic accident."

"Poor Joyce, she wasn't well-liked but I never thought her a thief," she replied. "At first I put it down to a delivery mistake but then I noticed items went missing after Wednesday nights. Little things like the odd cake or two but then it was expensive spices and decorations. I've put my heart into this business and all my life-savings."

"Were all your cinnamon brownies ruined today?"

"Yes, pretty much so. Fortunately people have been understanding. I'll just have to try again. I do feel guilty that the door wouldn't open but that's the design. I must look at getting it changed. But…"

Callie rubbed her forehead trying to remember something but the moment vanished when Helen and Mary burst into the room. They were still arguing about Joyce. "I still can't understand why she was in the store cupboard on her own? Why didn't she call out?"

"How could she? The woman slipped and hit her head. She was unconscious. The police said so." Mary's eyebrows shot up. Callie sensed her exasperation. She knew Mary liked things to be straight forward.

"Even so, I think it a bit odd." Helen said.

"That's enough!" Callie slapped her hand on the work top. The three women looked at her. They weren't used to her being so abrupt.

For once Callie didn't care what anyone thought. Her head was pounding, she wanted a warm bath and she still needed to do a stock check.

"It's not every day one finds a dead body in a store cupboard," Callie said firmly. "But I'm sure you will understand if I want to say goodnight to you all and thank you for looking in on me."

"Come along you two, Callie's right. We've taken up too much of her time and she needs some rest." Tina followed them out the door, flicking the closed sign round as she left.

Callie gave them a half-hearted wave and decided it was time to tackle the store cupboard. I'll have to face it again at some point I might as well get it over and done with she thought. The little room always smelled of warm freshly baked cakes, but now there was a whiff of disinfectant from the corner where Joyce had fallen. She had tried to clean up as soon as the police had finished.

She picked up some empty trays and counted the spice jars. She would get someone in to scrub the place properly from start to finish tomorrow and soon Callie's Cake Shop would be back to normal.

She looked down. A cinnamon brownie had rolled behind the shelf. She knelt to pick it up. She crumbled it between her fingers and breathed in the warm spicy aroma. She had been keen to try it out as a special edition cake. She did one every month but her first attempt at cinnamon brownies had been ruined. Joyce's death had seen to that.

A snatch of an earlier conversation about cinnamon came back to her. She realised she'd made a terrible mistake. Joyce had never been the thief.

She heard a soft tapping along the corridor. A voice called out. "Sorry Callie dear. I really don't want to do this but I thought it wouldn't be long before you worked it out."

A figure appeared at the store cupboard door holding a rolling pin. Callie felt her stomach tighten. She kept her voice light. "I'm sure we can talk about it and really it's just the odd cake or two."

"I know I did a terrible thing. The doctor said this compulsion to take things was sparked by the divorce and job loss. But I'm never going back to that place again for treatment…Never. How did you know it was me?"

"When you mentioned the tray of cinnamon brownies I knew you had been in the store cupboard that evening. Only Joyce and I knew I'd made those cakes, and I've just checked the spice box. Some jars are missing. Joyce denied being the thief when I confronted her. I'd returned to the shop after we'd shut for the day and found her rummaging through the boxes."

"She was probably checking supplies after she saw me slip out of there earlier," Tina said. "It was foolish to mention the brownies, though." Her voice rose and she edged forward. Callie knew she would be backed into a corner. She dived for the door just as Tina lunged forward with the rolling pin. Callie swung a tray to deflect the weapon. Tina lashed out again and Callie flung herself against her, forcing her to drop the rolling pin. The two women landed on the floor.

Her opponent was stronger than her slight frame appeared and Callie needed all her strength to keep her down. As they grappled on the floor a bag of flour toppled from a shelf. It burst in a shower over Tina who coughed and wheezed. Callie saw her chance to reach the door. Tina screeched and tried to grab her foot but Callie was too quick. She threw herself into the passageway and shoved her weight against the door.

Callie ignored Tina's hammering on the wooden frame. After a while there were a few feeble taps. Finally they stopped.

There could be only one star baker at her cake shop thought Callie as she set about baking more cinnamon brownies. She thought it a pity that Joyce had slipped and hit her head when she'd shut the cupboard door to teach her a lesson.

She made a note to change the lock on Monday. She'd had a lucky escape. It would be terrible to find herself trapped in there one day.

Stephen Massie has travelled extensively, experiencing many cultures. His interest in sailing originates from childhood. As a boy, standing on the beach at Mersea Island in England, he would fantasise about sailing out into the unknown on one of the Thames barges which sail quite close to the shore.

In the nineteen eighties he was an advanced automation engineer in the automotive industry. During this time he worked on and developed robotic machine intelligent vision systems. The combination of his sailing experiences plus his technical background inspired him to write the *When Dreams Converge* trilogy.

Foul Encounter

Solitude, a state which encourages reflection of one's past behaviours and failings, tends to sharpen the mind. Remorse can come to the most hardened heart, even for one who considers himself above the law. His thoughts were broken by a sudden change in wind direction as his brand new Macwester 26 yacht jerked hard to starboard throwing him to his knees. Darren Douglas looked a sorry sight on what should have been a joyous maiden voyage.

The purchase of the yacht signified his success, though he never imagined sailing her would be so difficult. Alone in the open waters of the Thames Estuary the reality of what he had done began to dawn on him. In a moment of unsuppressed anger Ria, his true love, was gone leaving him alone on the boat which he clearly could not control. She had made sailing seem so easy, but now amongst the dangerous shallows he was at the mercy of the elements. He wished he could start again, to be given a second chance.

Stealing came easy to him, driven by greed and a lack of concern for other people. The bank deposit box he had prised open on that cold November night last year was to change his life more than he could ever envisage. He remembered the bank vault sparkling from the light reflecting off the large cut diamond which lay inside the box. It was immediately obvious to him that it was worth thousands.

With his new-found wealth and subsequently meeting Ria just two months later, his life couldn't have been better. Her love of the sea was infectious and soon she persuaded him to buy the Macwester, which he insisted on naming after her. But whilst they waited for the boat to be built things changed, nothing obvious at first, but gradually happiness began to drain from their relationship. He convinced himself once they were aboard their new yacht all would be well.

Ria, a qualified coastal skipper, took the helm as they sailed from the coast of Sussex to their new home port of West Mersea in Essex. Any sign of strain between them evaporated as their adventure at sea began. Ria was clearly in charge of proceedings. "Women's lib," Darren had muttered to himself, ensuring she wouldn't hear him, "Where would it all end?" In the grand scheme of things men were still in the forefront of exploration, it was only last month that Neil Armstrong had been the first man to land on the moon.

With nothing much to do on deck he went below to make a cup of tea for both of them. Whilst waiting for the kettle to boil he consoled himself that one day he too would indeed learn to navigate and sail. He looked over to where a confusing array of charts and navigation instruments lay strewn across the highly polished mahogany saloon table. None of what he saw made much sense; unfamiliar calculations scribbled on pieces of paper and pencilled lines drawn across a chart. He pulled out the drawer which was mounted beneath the table. It was stuffed with even more charts and tide tables and as he tried to close it again it jammed, leaving it half open. There was something catching at the back. He forced his hand into the small gap between the underside of the table top and the drawer. Using just the tips of his outstretched fingers he soon found the source of the problem. Ignoring the sound of the kettle, which by this time was beginning to boil, he persevered in his endeavour to free the obstruction and soon pulled out an envelope. Darren's relief turned to one of concern as a cheque for one thousand pounds fell out of the envelope together with a letter which read,

"Thank you for tracking him down. Regards, Tini DeVirs."

That was all that was written, nine simple words that to him surely meant betrayal. He stormed out of the cabin. Ria's complexion immediately turned pale when she saw the cheque which Darren was waving in his hand. The unattended kettle's whistle continued to scream.

"I can explain," she began, but before she could continue Darren grabbed her throat. She gasped for air, trying in vain to pull his hands away.

"I know what you have done. Is that all I am worth to you?" Who is Tini DeVirs?" he ranted, easing his grip on her neck.

"I don't know; I have never met her," she whispered in a hoarse voice.

Fuming that he was being lied to, Darren squeezed harder and Ria's lips trembled then began to turn blue, as her eyes bulged. With all the strength she could muster she gasped, "You stole her diamond."

Furious, he tightened his grip, ignoring her pleading eyes, until every drop of life had been extinguished from the one he had once loved so much.

****

Drifting in the swirl of the tugging tide, a small fishing dinghy bobbed helplessly. Her sole occupant watched and waited for the blue hulled yacht he had spotted rising from the horizon to reach him. A bucket he had attached to a line to act as a makeshift sea anchor was proving to be of little help in the strong current. He knew if the oncoming boat did not provide assistance he would soon be pulled out into the depths of the North Sea.

But that wouldn't happen he reassured himself; help was on its way.

****

Darren panicked at the sight of Ria's limp body which lay at his feet. He had no idea where he was or how to control the boat. Ahead he saw the fishing boat. A man stood on the foredeck frantically waving at him; it was obvious he was in distress. Darren battled with his dilemma; should he continue with his struggle alone on the yacht or have the benefit of an experienced sailor aboard, thereby risking detection of Ria's murder. Unexpectedly the yacht lurched violently and with the sudden fright, his mind was made up. But what should he do with the body? Too close to be undetected he couldn't dispose of it over the side. He had to think fast; soon it would be too late. Grabbing Ria by the ankles he dragged her down from the cockpit, her head hitting the steps, and through to the front cabin, her long blonde hair trailing along the floor stained in blood seeping from her cracked skull. Without hesitation he quickly stuffed the body into a locker and slammed the door shut. Hastily he then wiped the floor to remove any trace of her being. He had to hurry for his yacht was almost upon the small craft.

****

Alarmed at the rapid descent of the bow looming above him, the man in the fishing boat was forced to fend the yacht off; it was clearly out of control.

"Grab the rope!" Darren yelled from the cockpit.

There was just enough time for the man to fasten one end to a stern cleat before the slack was taken up. The line twisted and the fishing boat turned sharply once the rope was under tension.

"What the hell are you doing?" was the cry from the stricken vessel.

"I can't control it. The wind is too strong."

Waves smashed into the stern of the little boat causing it to take on far too much water. She was now being dragged under by the yacht. Desperate to address the situation the man found himself in, he grabbed hold of the line spanning the two boats and pulled his way across. Up to his midriff in angry water he never felt the cold as he concentrated on his very survival. The fishing boat was rapidly disappearing beneath the waves. He struggled to make the last few feet, his outstretched arm grabbed by Darren as the weight of the sinking boat began to pull the yacht's stern down. Soon both vessels would be lost. With one last heave the stranger was aboard and before a word was spoken he sliced through the taut line with a sharp knife he found lying on a locker. The sudden release caused the yacht to rise sharply, throwing both men to the floor.

"What sort of idiot are you? My boat, it's gone!"

Darren did not take kindly to being spoken to in this manner. Snatching the knife from the man's hand he glared at him then, sensing the tension, his new acquaintance attempted to alleviate the anger.

"I am sorry. It was just a bit of a shock. Thank you for rescuing me."

Darren remained silent.

"I'm Simon Winter and you are?" he said, offering his hand as he looked up to the large stocky brute, still holding the knife in a threatening manner.

"Never mind who I am. Can you sail?" Darren growled.

"I can," he replied cautiously, afraid of provoking this aggressive looking man any further, "And you?"

"It's my first time."

"You can't sail?"

"No," Darren replied, his face appearing a little calmer, "And I have no idea where we are."

Thinking it best not to pry any further Simon told him that they were in the East Swin channel just off the Gunfleet sandbanks.

"Are we close to Mersea Island?" Darren replied.

"Not far. Is that where you are headed?"

"Yes," Darren said as he sheathed the knife and placed it in his jacket pocket.

Simon let out a small sigh before continuing, "Okay, first things first. You will have to help me change tack. At present we are heading in the wrong direction."

After several painstaking minutes with Simon explaining to Darren how and when to manoeuvre the foresail, they were ready to change course. As Simon pulled the weathered heavy oak tiller to port, 'Ria' responded by turning towards starboard. Both her tan sails began to crack and flap in the wind which was now coming directly towards her bow. Simon took up the slack on her mainsail sheets as Darren worked in front of him on her foresail. The boom swung across, missing their heads by inches, then within moments the yacht had heeled and was ploughing through the waves in a broad reach.

"Take the helm and keep her on a course of 220 degrees," Simon ordered, pointing towards the compass situated on top of the wooden cabin hatch.

"I'll be below calculating our course from my last known position."

"No, don't do that; I'm not sure I can manage to steer an accurate course. I need you here with me."

"Sure you can. Besides, if we wander a little it won't matter," Simon said as he started his descent into the cabin.

Darren was unsure what to do; there was no way of stopping him. He should have taken his chances alone at sea. It would be obvious once Simon got below that someone else had been on board. He had no choice; his right hand reached for the knife in his jacket pocket. As soon as he let go of the tiller it flew across, causing the yacht to turn away from the wind. With all his strength he pulled the tiller back.

"Are you concentrating on what you are doing?" called out Simon from the cabin.

This was useless, he couldn't let go. Then noticing a length of cord tied to a rail beside him, he lashed the tiller with the cord to reduce its movement. Tentatively he released his grip and when satisfied his fix had worked, he made his way down towards Simon.

Simon stood quite still before the saloon table with his back to his would be assailant. Darren crept nearer raising the knife high above his head. With one downward blow it would soon be over. Simon felt the warm breath on the back of his neck.

"Tired virgins make dull company," he announced.

"What?" Darren replied, distracted for a moment from his murderous task.

"It's a way of remembering True, Variation, Magnetic, Deviation and Compass. Something I know you don't understand however," he said, slowly turning towards Darren, who froze in his tracks at the sight of the powerful looking hand gun in Simon's grasp. "Ria did. Now please lower your arm and place that rather crude knife on the table."

Darren did as he was told then enquired, "I don't understand; who are you?"

"I have been waiting to rendezvous with you. It appears you have disposed of my accomplice, Ria. I am right - you have killed her?"

 Darren nodded.

"Pity, she was very good at tracking down people. Miss Tini DeVirs will not be happy to have lost her."

"Who is this Tini DeVirs?"

"I can say she is not the sort of person you would want to steal from," he smiled, "Oh, but you have.

And now I am afraid you will have to pay the price."

"Please, no. Who is she? Mafia? Perhaps I could work for her and repay my debt."

"Miss DeVirs is very particular who she employs."

Darren looked down at the gun, trying to come to terms with the fact that there was no way out for him, but through sheer instinct he turned to run. The blast when it came resounded throughout the yacht. He slumped to the floor, his eyes fixed in a stare towards his cold blooded assassin.

"No hard feelings, my dear fellow; it was just business."

You can discover further adventures aboard 'Ria' and who Tini DeVirs was by reading Stephen Massie's suspense thriller trilogy:

When Dreams Converge

Sleeper

Awaken

Sylvia Kent is a long established Essex writer specialising in non-fiction and journalism. Very active in the world of writing, she works with the Brentwood Writers' Circle and The Society of Women Writers & Journalists (where she holds the position of archivist). She speaks publically about writing and is a regular on such as Phoenix FM.

So, it is perhaps appropriate to end this anthology with a contribution from someone who has long written about Essex. This piece (enabled by Sylvia's position as a trustee of Cater Museum) describes the building in Harwich of a replica of the famous ship the *Mayflower;* it is intended that the ship will make a voyage to USA in 2020.

ESSEX CONNECTIONS WITH THE NEW WORLD

Many Essex history enthusiasts have already begun planning their September 2020 celebrations in tandem with their America counterparts. There has always been a huge interest in the ancient quay on the banks of the Thames that played a vital part in the early history of the emigrants to the new World in the 17th century. In today's modern atlases, dozens of Essex towns and villages share similar name links with America.

Setting Sail

Long before the momentous voyage of the Mayflower setting sail from Plymouth on 6 September 1620, we know there had been several earlier attempts to land on what is now known as America.

The first was Sir Walter Raleigh's Charter from Queen Elizabeth 1 to colonise Virginia, the area of North America named after the 'Virgin Queen'. In 1585 Raleigh attempted to convert a naval base at Roanoake Island into a settled colony. When war with the Spanish cut off communications with England, the settlers were left to fend for themselves. Sadly, when a relief expedition arrived in 1590, there was no trace of the settlers. The mystery as to what happened to those first pioneers endures to this day.

The Second Expedition

The next endeavour to conquer the New World took place in 1606. Three small ships sailed from London's Blackwall pier. Forty crew were on board alongside 105 settlers including a clergyman, twenty nine gentlemen, four carpenters, a blacksmith, bricklayer, mason, surgeon, twelve labourers and four boys. No women joined the expedition. We know that at least eleven of those early settlers came from Essex, more than from any other county. Under the overall command of Captain Christopher Newport from Harwich (1561-1617), the ships Godspeed, Discovery and Susan Constant, began their journey to the unknown. London's Virginia Company was the sponsor for financing the prospective voyage to these unmapped foreign shores. The great plan was three-fold: to discover the legendary north-west route to China; bring Christianity to the inhabitants of those foreign lands and underlying all, was the alluring possibility of discovering gold.

Sailing via the West Indies, and with fresh supplies, Captain Newport and his crew, the vessels arrived in Chesapeake Bay on 26 April 1607. Within a few weeks, the colonists established a base they named Jamestown. This was to honour their new king, James 1 who had been crowned in London in 1603. More of the Jamestown settlers came from Essex than from any other English county.

They faced many difficulties, terrible harvests resulting in the 'starving time', constant Indian attacks, and unrest within the colony. Illness from malaria killed many. Thanks to the perseverance and courage of those first pioneers, Jamestown survived and is celebrated in the USA as 'the first successful English settlement in the New World – indeed, it is also quoted as 'the Cradle of the Nation'.

The Mayflower Sails

Thirteen years later on 16 September 1620, another expedition set sail from Plymouth. The ship carrying them was the Mayflower with 102 passengers aboard, again many from Essex. John Carver of Braintree chartered the vessel. Christopher Jones of Harwich was Master and Samuel Fuller from Ockendon was ship's doctor. Great Burstead was the home of at least five of the Mayflower's passengers with Christopher Martin providing the supplies. His home still stands in Billericay High Street. These religious visionaries set out to make their homes in a new world, free from religious persecution. They landed at Cape Cod, Massachusetts sixty six days later. Unfortunately, most of the Billericay newcomers and others on the manifest died within weeks of their arrival in America.

Legendary Essex links

Essex was a strong recruiting ground for the Colonies. Descendants from many of the county's families, particularly those originating in Dedham, Chelmsford and Braintree are listed. The Sherman family have traced their descendants as founders of Rhode Island, while another was General W T Sherman of the American Civil War. Braintree produced John Adams, the second president of the

US and his son, who became the sixth. Presidential connections are found in Purleigh, where Lawrence, the Great-great-grandfather of the first American president, George Washington, was minister during the mid-1660s. Lawrence is buried in Maldon's All Saints Church. Ancestors of the Bush family can be found at Messing and Feering from the 14th century. Reynold Bush emigrated during the 1630s, possibly on The Lyon.

The celebrated Thomas Hooker was appointed Town Lecturer and Curate at St Mary's Church, Chelmsford in the 1620s. However, the parish censured his Puritan beliefs. He emigrated in 1633 to America and today is remembered for co-founding the State of Connecticut. Brentwood was another place from which religious souls also said goodbye to family and friends to seek a new life. In 1635, Thomas Wright, son of the Brentwood squire, John Wright of Marygreen Manor, also packed his sea trunk and sailed on the ship Susan and Ellen. They made for Old Bay, Massachusetts and eventually settled at Watertown near Boston.

Our present Lord Petre whose childhood was spent at Ingatestone Hall, writes much about his noble ancestors, particularly Robert James, 8th Lord Petre (1713-1742). This family member's contribution to horticulture is legendary. He met the distinguished American botanist John Bartrum of Philadelphia on a trip in the 1730s. Bartrum supplied cuttings and seeds of numerous varieties of American trees planted at Thorndon Hall, near Brentwood. These were unknown in England at the time. Many years later, Lady Petre who was living at Thorndon, sent pear and apple seeds to cuttings to a friend in Philadelphia. Many of the trees planted almost 300 years ago, can be found in Thorndon Park today.

<u>War Years</u>

During the outbreak of the War of American Independence, the local regiments of the 44th and 56th (later to become the Essex Regiment) sailed to the USA. Landing in 1775, they took part in numerous battles and in 1780, they were transferred to Canada, staying there until 1786.

<u>First Flight</u>

In 1903, descendants of John Wright of Brentwood, namely Wilbur and Orville Wright – made history by flying the first 'heavier than air' biplane. The airfield was at Kitty Hawk, North Carolina.

<u>Industry</u>

The American motor magnate, Henry Ford had been contemplating opening a new factory in Essex for several years. In 1924 he completed his purchase of 144 acres of Dagenham marshland from Samuel Williams at Dagenham Dock. Ford's plan to build a huge car plant along the Thames foreshore became reality. He and his wife paid a flying visit in 1928 and the following year, his only son, Edsel, then president of this American firm, cut the first turf with a silver spade. Thousands of workers arrived in this small town, changing its character and size forever. In 1931, the first vehicles rolled off the assembly line and the Ford Motor Company was launched.

American GIs

The Second World War had been going since 1939 and to assist Britain, thousands of American servicemen and women arrived in the county in 1942. They increased the 23 air-bases already located in Essex, all of which were speedily built.

Town Twinning

The idea of matching towns purely for friendship across the Atlantic has been a favourite topic for many councils in Essex. From the end of World War II, numerous Town Twinning Associations have been created, and still maintain, important America-Essex links. Visits, particularly from scholars from both countries have been popular and many agree that this is a superb way of learning about their sister towns.

Essex enjoys a fascinating heritage with important historical links with America. Overseas visitors enjoy paying visits to the towns and villages they played such a vital part in both countries provenance. High on the list, is the Stour Valley, whose landscape inspired the world-famous artist John Constable who lived at Flatford. Nearby Dedham was the place of his education and is now regarded as 'Constable Country'. The 400th anniversary of the founding of Jamestown in 1606 has lead to a series of activities which has strengthened the relationship between the folk of Essex and America. This has included a trade mission from Essex to Virginia and the promotion of Essex as a tourist destination.

The Future

The story doesn't end there. Members of the Harwich Mayflower Project are building an authentic replica of the ship that carried the Pilgrims to America to a better life in the New World. In 2020 the new Mayflower will embark on a new and crucial journey that will carry today's Adventurers as they face up to the environmental dangers and challenges presented by climate change. This is a project that will inspire, provoke and deliver personal transformation, strategic local regeneration, community resilience and global co-operation. Are you an Adventurer? Why not join them? www.harwichmayflowerproject.com

"Twenty years from now you will be more disappointed by the things you didn't do than by the ones you did do. So throw off the bowlines. Sail away from the safe harbour. Catch the trade winds in your sails.
Explore. Dream. Discover." – Mark Twain

Rick O'Brien is an early-retired teacher.

Some years ago he wrote and illustrated *East Anglian Curiosities*, a comprehensive guide to all that is most remarkable or curious in Norfolk, Suffolk and Essex; part of a series covering the whole of England by the Dovecote Press. He was inspired to write this short story by his chapter on Zeppelin raids over Essex.

Rick is now working on what he hopes will be his first novel for junior readers.

He enjoys caravanning and gardening and is married with two children and lives in Norfolk.

Little Wigborough's Big Night

Doing any form of cleaning often left me disappointed with the result. So when my turn came to scrub Little Wigborough's Zeppelin Memorial, on its tenth anniversary, I let out a steamy sigh as I faced the object and the task.

The memorial sat opposite our cottage at the side of the lane very near to where the airship crashed. My best intention was to leave the concrete cross respectfully presentable and clearly visible and attractive to passers-by. The bronze plaque at the base had dulled and weathered since its last polish and was almost obliterated by cobwebs and mud splashed up by cars and tractors. That familiar list of names deserved at least to bathe in the sun's rays.

'Special Constable Edgar Nicholas, Police Constable Charles Smith . . .' ten names in all, and my favourite inscription at the end:

'For Distinguished Effort,

Robert Neave, aged 11.'

In bed that night of the 23rd September 1916, my deep dreaming was smashed like a shattering window pane. "Rob, Rob. Wake up quickly, son. Get your coat on," said Dad, shaking my shoulder vigorously. "We've got to go."

"What's happening, Dad? It must be the middle of the night."

"Look out your window."

I did as he asked, as always.

I rubbed the sleep from my half-opened eyes, pulled the coat from the bed and put it on over my pyjamas.

In that half-moon sky there lurked something enormous and menacing, a massive mechanical cloud that drifted slowly towards our row of cottages. "What is it, Dad?"

"A German airship I believe. But there's to be no lingering, son," and he grabbed my coat sleeve and hauled me through the bedroom door. "Get a move on."

I felt the power of his insistence as he prodded my back all the way down the stairs. Mum and my two younger sisters Emily and Florence, holding a doll each, were already gathered by the back door, having speedily dressed in their coats and hats.

Mum called out as soon as she saw me. "Hurry, Robert," and she beckoned, "No time for shoes."

We bolted through the back door like lambs chased by a yelping sheepdog. Behind me I heard the monster's engine – the bark of the collie. Mum ran with a sister firmly gripped in each hand. She loyally followed Dad down the narrow path and through the wooden gate at the far end of the garden that shattered as he thrust it aside in his haste. I gave it a kick as I passed.

I stopped and turned to look at the angry monster as it had ceased growling and appeared suspended in mid-air right in front of our cottage. Did they intend to bomb our house?

Dad shouted, "Keep running, Rob. We're not clear yet."

We sprinted and clawed our way through an almost pitch black wheat field. Wisps of grass slashed at my face and a dewy smell of crushed seeds reminded me of school dinners. Somewhere far off I heard Rusty, our terrier, barking. I whistled but he never came.

"That's far enough," Dad said when we reached the edge of the field. We sat, gasping for some cool night air. My feet throbbed and I picked wheat seeds from under my toenails and between my toes. Emily cried her feet hurt so much.

Mum asked, "Is our home safe? Will that thing explode?"

"It's hard to say, Mother. The airship appears damaged and there could even be bombs aboard," Dad replied. "In which case there'd be an almighty explosion. Evil creations, Zeppelins."

Again, I heard Rusty in the distance, doing his job– keeping guard. My eyes fixed on the stricken airship as it descended into the field opposite our cottage. Echoes of grinding metal reverberated through the air as it flopped to the ground like a person fainting. My legs felt the tremor when the craft landed, without exploding. Mum reached out and pulled Emily and Florence close to her. I expected the gas-filled airship to burst into flames at any moment.

Dad was no longer with us so I dashed off, ignoring Mum. "Robert, don't go, son. Don't leave us here," she called as I located our path through the crop.

Arriving at the cottage, I found the back door open wide. I crept inside. In the dark front room, a cigarette dangling from his mouth, Dad stood motionless, staring out of the window at the threat lingering in the field. Its back had broken.

"A hundred more feet and we'd have been flattened," he said, without turning round.

"I've come back for Rusty."

"Rusty can take care of himself, son. It's the Germans we need to deal with. That crew have survived the crash. I can see them milling around the pilot's cabin. We're going to need help."

I noticed a kitchen knife in his right hand when it fleetingly reflected the bright half-moon. "We were told at school that the Germans ate children."

"Unlikely, son, unlikely, but they'll be desperate not to get caught."

"We should hide."

He darted round the house checking that the doors and windows were locked. "Let's stay in the kitchen," he said, and he put the knife down and picked up a rolling pin. "I'll not let them near you, son," he said, waving the weapon towards the airship. "If they come . . ."

He was a brave dad. He'd have joined his pals in France as soon as war started if it wasn't for him having only one eye – he lost the other at school when a cricket ball hit it and killed his sight. He told the recruitment officer of the Essex Regiment that he could aim a gun with his one good eye, but they wouldn't sign him up. He was very disappointed but Mum was pleased. Other mothers had lost husbands.

I sat down at the dining table but immediately returned to my feet in response to loud banging on the front door by what sounded like a rifle butt. "You'd think they'd use the knocker," Dad said as flashlights sent multi-coloured piercing rays through the stained glass in our front door.

I was surprised at my shaking and steadied myself by holding the back of a chair as another round of banging ensued. "Is anyone inside? I am Captain Bocker of Zeppelin L33." The voice, in almost perfect English, had only a slight foreign accent. "Hello. Are you at home?"

"Don't answer," Dad whispered.

"What do you want?" I called out. Dad puffed up his cheeks and his eyebrows moved closer together as he raised a finger to his lips to signal silence.

"I am captain of the airship I have landed in your field. It is damaged and cannot fly any further. I must warn you – we intend to set fire to the airship. It could make a big explosion and injure your home. You have to get clear. Can you please hear me?"

Dad whispered again, "Rob, get your bike and pedal as fast as you can to Peldon post office. Wake the postmaster and ask him to call out the constable. Got that?" I nodded as I put my shoes on, then grabbed my cycle and pushed it down the back garden path and through the gate to join the lane just beyond the cottages. I could bearly make out the roadway in the subtle moonlight. As I got up to a good speed I rang my bell to let Dad know I was on my way when a bullet passed my head and hit a tree.

I didn't make it to Peldon. On the lane I met another cyclist coming the opposite way. We managed to stop on a sharp bend with screeching brakes, narrowly missing each other. The tall and rotund stranger dismounted and shone a torch light directly into my eyes. I tried to puzzle out who else might be on the road so early in the morning. I thought my fellow traveller might be a German agent racing to rescue his buddies.

"Who goes there?" asked the stranger. "Is it you young Neave, from the New Hall Farm cottages?"

"Yes sir, it's me, Robert."

"And I'm me, Robert – Special Constable Nicholas. I hear a Zeppelin's landed near your cottage without even asking permission . . ."

". . . Would you please stop pointing your lamp in my face, constable?"

"Oh, do excuse me."

"My dad's keeping an eye on them Germans – literally. Their captain said he will explode the airship and that we were to get clear."

"I've been watching the southern skyline for any sign of fire or smoke. Didn't see any."

"One of them shot at me."

"Really? What impudence! We can't have that, can we? Can you take me to the scene Robert and we'll see what can be done?"

Special Constable Nicholas failed to keep up with me and I arrived at the cottages a full ten minutes ahead of him. Ditching my cycle, I crawled along a boggy drainage trench by the side of our lane and got close to the wrecked airship without being seen. I didn't want to be shot at again.

I heard foreign voices, looked up and saw over a dozen men in navy uniform running in and out of the captain's cabin, which had nestled itself soundly on the ground like a parked automobile with the entire airship almost on top of it. They were carrying items from the airship, of which I now had a clear view as the early dawn emerged. It looked almost intact apart from a large dent in its back about half way along. Some of the outer canvas had been torn in places. If this weapon fell into English hands it would be a great victory.

Someone blew a whistle and the crew lined up before marching, in a very solid line, to the hedgerow at the side of the field and disappearing into the thicket.

It was at this moment I heard Rusty barking again. His voice seemed to come from inside the wrecked monster. I popped my head up from the muddy trench and saw Rusty scampering about right outside the airship's cabin. I recalled the captain telling us of his intention to set fire to his airship, but Rusty didn't know that.

A whistle might attract gunfire so I threw stones in Rusty's direction. That made him bark even more. Then a flare of yellow and blue shot out from where the German crew were hiding in the hedgerow. It seemed, like my stones, to have been aimed at Rusty but it bounced off the field and entered the cabin where it eventually fizzled out. Gunpowder smoke lingered in the still dawn air. It must have been sorrowful for the crew – attempting the destruction of their precious ship.

Another flare entered the vessel, and another. Rusty stood his ground as more flares hit the ship. Why did it not explode?

Crawling out of my trench and keeping as flat to the ground as I could, I dragged myself by my elbows towards my dog. All the while the Germans continued their bombardment of flares which shrieked above my head. It was like bonfire night or the Somme – which I read about daily in the newspaper. Each shot forced me to duck and bury my face in the mud. Before me spread a sort of no man's land into which I had to venture to rescue my pal, Rusty. It was a duty I felt unable to resist.

I knew time was not on my side. I stood up, ran towards my cherished pet and called, "Rusty, Rusty. Come here you old fool." Sure enough he heard and scampered towards me, jumped into my arms with a wagging tale and licked my face. Flares hit the ground and whizzed about us so close we could have toasted bread in their wake.

For a moment I lost my bearings and headed towards the Germans. But Rusty licked me awake and I turned and headed for my trench, almost reaching it when, behind me, the umpteenth flare set the airship alight. It burned rapidly with a heat so intense that Rusty's tail and the back of my coat were singed before we reached the protection of the ditch. But intense heat passed over us sucking the air from our lungs.

Incredibly, the airship did not explode but burnt in minutes leaving just its metal skeleton exposed. Rusty and I, covered in mud and licking our wounds, perched on the front doorstep facing the lane. Dad had joined us and he stood in the doorway, smoking.

Special Constable Nicholas finally arrived on his meandering bicycle, dismounted and gazed at the captain and his crew marching up the lane towards him. Raising an authoritative hand in the typical police manner, the constable halted the crewmen. "And where do you think you are off to?" he demanded of Captain Bocker.

"We are seeking directions to the port of Mersea, your lordship."

"Oh, are you now? Well I'm not giving you directions to the sea just so you can escape. But you can have directions to my lockup at Peldon post office. It's just up the lane."

He paused and looked over to me. "And Robert," he shouted through a cupped hand, "Make sure you and that hound get cleaned up next time we have guests."

At that, the crewmen put their hands on their heads and, with the Special Constable pushing his bicycle along beside them, marched all the way to Peldon and captivity.

SJ Banham is a writer with a career spanning some 30 years. She lives in Essex running her own business 'For The Love of Books' providing creative writing services including ghost writing and coaching.

Her seventh book, *I've Got A Pen & I'm Not Afraid To Use It* was published a year ago and can be ordered from www.loveofbooks.co.uk

The Client

My journey to this meeting had been uncomfortable. I'd travelled almost two hours for a trip that ought to have been forty-five minutes. For the most part, I had driven towards a storm and for the last ten miles, it hit. I was driving through torrential rain, thunder and lightning that would frighten even Thor himself. To add insult to injury, there were two sections of road works resulting in loose chippings against my windscreen and the route took me past an airfield for light aircraft. I didn't enjoy low flying planes at the best of times.

My meeting was with a potential client. I was approached via my website several weeks previously by a young woman named Stacy who wanted to hire me to ghost write her life story. From the state of her emails, she was not big on spelling, grammar or time as words were missed within sentences and it was up to the reader to understand the meaning. She had said she was an abused child and her parents were now arrested so she was 'free' to tell her story. Professionally, due to the type of life she'd lived, she wasn't my usual kind of client. This seemed surrounded with potential legal issues and a harrowing story. But, I try not to judge a client's needs before I meet with them, that way I am able to ascertain all the variables in a face to face meeting. Reading between the lines on the screen is one thing but reading between them via body language is an art all of its own.

Car parked, skirt straightened and cool drink purchased I sat at a table facing the front of the café. This, I generally found, was the best view for the client to see me and vice versa. The meeting was for 2pm, I had arrived at 1.30 and it was now 2.30pm. It was fast looking like a no-show and I decided to get out my purse to buy another drink before I called it a day. As I leaned down for my bag, a man approached me. He was smartly dressed in a suit as though he was away from the office at lunch time. He was tall and slim with attractive feature and his dark hair was parted on the left. He looked about thirty years old.

"Gina?" he asked. I must've looked puzzled but I nodded. "I'm …er..Stacy."

Confused, as I'd presumed I was meeting a woman, I slowly put out my hand to shake his. "Hello."

"You were expecting a girl, weren't you?"

"Stacy?" I smile, hoping I hadn't misread the emails. "Can I get you a coffee?"

He sat down in front of me but declined the drink with a wave of his hand. "It's not my real name."

At that point two things crossed my mind, was he for real and why was he giving out fake names? My face must have shown my confusion.

"I didn't think you'd see me if I told you I was male." For some gut reason, at this point the hairs went up on the back of my neck. He added, "I've been following your work for a while now. "I've been very impressed with all you do. I listen to your radio show too."

I didn't know how to respond other than to joke about how I felt so I giggled, "Oh, cool! You know you've made it in life when you have a stalker!"

"I'm Aiden," he laughed, "Aiden Miller."

I believed him instantly as was my nature but I shouldn't have been so quick to believe someone who had already lied to me.

"So, Aiden, are you interested in writing your own story or do you actually need a ghost writer?"

He seemed distant, he was thinking. He looked around the café at the growing queue and smiled, ignoring my question. "Bit too long to wait for a coffee now, eh? Perhaps we should wait until it goes down a bit."

I recalled in Stacy's emails that she – he, Aiden, had said he wasn't up to writing his own story due to time constraints and mental health issues. I lived with depression myself so it wasn't down to me to judge him. I wondered if his were due to the abuse he had suffered at the hands of his parents, if indeed that was the truth. Then it shot through my head that Aiden and Stacy were different people. I began to feel more confused than Aiden.

I tried again, "So do you enjoy writing?"

"I enjoy *your* writing. I've read your books. I particularly loved the one about the detective in America."

I'd written two about detectives in America so I quizzed him a little. "Which one did you prefer?"

"The one with the writer and the detective in Boston. Jayne and Tim."

My heart sank. He really did know my work. "Guardian Angel," I nodded. "What did you like about it?"

"The murders."

My eyebrows shot up in the air and I suppressed a laugh. "Any particular characters in that story jump out at you?"

"Jayne. She was based on you, wasn't she? I can tell."

I tipped my head to one side. "That's nothing out of the ordinary for a writer to do," I explained. She wasn't based on me. Parts of her personality were but essentially she was completely fiction. I tried hard to keep the feeling light and remain professional but there was something not quite right about the whole set up. Who in their right mind concocts a story, changes their name and shows up late to a meeting that could so easily have been straightforward?

"I love her tattoo," he said softly, looking straight at me. "I'd love to see it sometime."

The way he spoke made me feel a little too exposed. The character of Jayne had a tattoo of a cartoon devil on her shoulder – I did not, mostly because I was not Jayne. Now I felt very uncomfortable. Was he flirting or just incredibly creepy? I was still unsure so moved the conversation back to why we were meeting.

"So, the story you emailed me about, is it for real?"

"Partially," he nodded.

"Which part?"

"The abuse."

"OK." My mind was racing down different avenues of questioning. "Is it something you want to write about because it happened to you or someone you know?"

"Someone I know."

Suddenly the chatty Aiden on email had grown cold and become very economical with his words. I decided to try a different approach.

"Generally when a potential client asks for a meeting, it is because they are unsure whether they want to hire a ghost writer or maybe because they want to write the story themselves but are unsure how to go about it so I help by being their writing coach. Sometimes it is completely different and they don't have a story at all but until they discuss it at length, they don't know that. The point is that if they don't have a story to be written but an event actually did happen, it is possible just speaking about it can help in a therapeutic and cathartic way. Do you think that might be the case here?"

Aiden didn't respond to the question. Then he looked up at the diminished queue and said, "I think I will have a drink now." Then he got up and headed for the counter.

I was confused. What was this about? What was going on here? My imagination was racing and I was wondering if this was about to be the weirdest and most non-productive meeting I'd ever had or if Aiden was a crazed murderer and I was his next victim. Of course, my imagination was expert at conjuring the most exciting story from just a few words or actions so imagining Aiden was up to no good was as easy as pie. If I was honest with myself I could look at the Barista serving him and assume the young girl of about eighteen was, in her free time, a lawyer in training, a pole-dancer, mother of three, a mechanic in training or about to join a nunnery.

Finally Aiden sat down. He had bought himself a pot of tea and set about prodding the tea bag in the pot with his spoon.

"The person who was abused was a cousin of mine."

"Was?"

"She died."

"I'm sorry to hear that, Aiden." I had to be careful with my questioning and choice of words. "How old was she when the abuse began?"

"Fifteen," he said, sipping at his tea, "it stopped when she was eighteen and she died."

"What did she die of?"

"She was murdered."

I felt my stomach knot up and I went cold. "Murdered? When was this?"

"A few months ago."

"It's still very fresh then," I said, hoping to offer a mixture of sympathy and professionalism. "Perhaps you need to absorb the whole saga first before you write about it. Besides there are other family members to think about; her parents, for instance. If you write with the intention of publishing, you will need to consider their feelings. Plus, presumably, the police are crawling all over it?

"Cut and dried with the police and her parents gave her up. She lived with me."

I tried to read between the lines. Was he saying he felt guilty for not preventing her abuse and subsequent murder or was he confessing to it?

"Then I have to tell you now that professionally, I wouldn't touch this as it is too close time-wise and is a potential legal nightmare. My advice to you is if you want to write about it then don't publish it, but if you do write about it, be very, very careful. Like I said, my professional advice is not to touch it at all."

"That surprises me," his demeanour seemed angered now. "Jayne virtually watched a murderer carry out their crime."

I sighed. "Jayne Murray is and was a fictional character, Aiden, in a fictional book. It was all made up. Out of my imagination."

"I should be honest with you, shouldn't I?"

I felt my throat dry up. My eyes were likely wide with anxiety but the café was filling up a little so my security was potentially alright. "I would appreciate that."

"I wanted to meet you. I follow your work and I listen to your shows and I know a lot about you. I know a lot more about you than you probably know."

I swallowed hard trying to remain composed. Inside I was actually terrified.

"I don't want to write about the abuse, I want you to."

"I don't think this story is for me, Aiden. If I'm truthful." I saw the disappointment on his face and it frightened me. The potential of what he may be capable of scared me. I wondered if he was excited by the kind of fear he was filling me with. Was this what happened to his cousin?

"I may be able to refer you to another writer who can help but to be honest, getting anybody to write publicly about something this fresh and with the legal attention surrounding it might be really difficult. I am just being up-front with you. I hope you understand."

Aiden pushed away his teapot and cup now it was drained. "Oh I do understand, but I'm not giving up that easily."

I saw a coldness in his eyes. Something inside him was missing but I didn't know what. A soul, maybe? I just knew the man in front was creeping the hell out of me and only my professionalism was keeping me here.

"Well, that might be a good thing. Tenacity can be a good trait." I wrote down the name of an acquaintance of mine, another writer but one who had a background of working in the police force. If anyone knew anything about judging the character of people, it was Jamie Westbridge. I tore the name from the page and handed the now curled piece of paper to him. "This guy also lives in Essex. He's been a writer for years. I will email him and let him know about you. He may be in touch. How does that sound?"

Aiden took the scrap of paper and nodded. "I won't forget this, Gina," he said.

I took that in a pleasant way thought my gut told me otherwise. I smiled and put out my hand to shake his. "It has been interesting meeting you. I hope your project works out."

Aiden stood, shook my hand and smiled. As I put away my notebook he left the café abruptly.

I watched him vanish and then quickly took out my phone to email Jamie. I gave him the particulars and pressed send.

Somehow I knew that wouldn't be the last of any dealings with Aiden but even if I was involved somehow, I knew that Jamie would be watching in the wings and ready to stop anything bad before it began.

I left the café and headed towards the car park analysing the meeting during my five minute journey. As I approached the car park, I could see my car and next to it was a tall dark figure. It was Aiden Miller.

Sue Butler currently lives on the east coast of Essex, close to a creek and salt-marsh. She is Poetry Editor of Writers' Forum magazine, www.writers-forum.com.

She also produces a monthly poetry feature for the internationally renowned, Beth Chatto Garden (www.bethchatto.co.uk) and is responsible for the creative writing exercise in Wetherspoon News.

A keen walker and gardener, Sue works as a copywriter specialising in health & wellbeing. Her particular interest is in the psychological elements people can harness to ensure they lose weight quickly and safely then don't regain it.

Hungry

Emma takes three deeps breaths then forces herself to close the fridge door. She walks to the large, butler sink, turns on the cold tap and lets the water run for a while before she fills a tall glass. She drinks until the glass is empty, fills it again, drinks half and has to stop. She sits at the kitchen table watching the clock on the pine dresser count away the minutes... seven... nine... ten. *No,* Emma says aloud, *what I'm feeling isn't thirst.*

Emma shuts her eyes, rubs her face with her hands then gets up and searches in a drawer of the pine dresser for a pen and some paper. She sits back down at the kitchen table and records the date and time at the top of the sheet of paper. She holds the pen ready to write. *How do I feel?* she asks herself aloud. *How do I really feel?* She is not at all sure and this worries her. She shakes her head despondently and asks herself, *Am I genuinely hungry or am I using food to fill a hole in my life? Am I bored, lonely or resentful about something? Am I using food to smother a fear or to avoid facing an unpleasant truth? Am I disappointed?*

As Emma ponders the options, she reaches over and opens the fridge door. Without leaving her chair, she allows her left hand to venture into the fridge. As she asks herself, *Am I angry?* she tears a leg off the roasted, corn-fed, free-range chicken. She knows the salt-rubbed skin is where most of the calories lurk but she eats it anyway. Still chewing chicken, she drops the leg bone, grabs a wedge of Parmesan and takes a huge, almost savage bite. She looks briefly at her teeth marks before taking another bite and another.

Emma forgets about the paper and turns her chair to face the fridge. She grabs more chicken, opens a jar of mayonnaise and drinks it. She eats pâté, schnitzel, five pork sausages wrapped in smoked bacon, all the sage-and-onion stuffing, some potato dauphinoise, four hard-boiled duck eggs, half a spinach quiche, a lemon torte, two tubs of humus, eight pickled walnuts, twelve profiteroles, some pecan pie, over a pint of whipped, Chantilly cream, capers, olives, marron glacés and a whole packet of salted butter. In too much of a hurry to find a spoon, she uses her hands to scoop up trifle full of brandy-soaked sponge and cherries dipped in white, Belgian chocolate.

Exhausted, Emma starts crying. Her stomach hurts and to ease the pain she drinks Riesling from the bottle. *I know it cost over fifteen pounds,* she sobs, *but I need it. I do.* When the bottle is empty, she tells it, *I'd like to fill a bath and sink this body I hate into scalding water. But even if I close the blind and don't turn on the light, I can't bear to see my enormous, bloated, stomach, my flabby breasts and thighs – everywhere cellulite.* Emma sits crying until she hears her husband's car on the drive.

She hauls herself up, closes the fridge door and tidies up the debris as best she can in the time available. She hides the empty wine bottle under shirts in the laundry basket. *I meant to iron you earlier this afternoon,* she tells the shirts, *but some days it's a struggle to get out of bed let alone get all the jobs done.* She wipes her face on a tea towel, a souvenir from Edinburgh Castle.

Her husband puts down his briefcase and, before he can even greet her, Emma tells him, *I've not had time to go shopping, so we'll have to eat out.* He starts to say he will be happy with leftovers from the supper they had last night with friends. Then he notices Emma's tearstained face; the food stains on her blouse and skirt; the way she is standing, hands on her hips, as if she is ready for a fight. He counts slowly to five in his head then says, *Going out will be nice. How do you feel about Italian?*

Emma's husband goes upstairs. He takes his time changing his clothes; wishes the simple task could take a day, a week. After hanging up his suit, he stands in his blue, cotton boxer shorts in front of the mirror. He tells his reflection, *Damn it. I don't have to live like this. I'm a decent catch. Even with this paunch, I'm sure plenty of women would look at me twice; would sleep with me and not be ashamed to tell their friends, boast about it even.* He sees clearly the new life he could live.

He thinks about packing a bag, climbing out the window onto the extension roof, sliding down the drainpipe and walking away - no looking back. For a moment, it seems possible. But the moment passes. *I'll stay for now,* he tells his reflection, *but not forever.* The thought cheers him immensely. When he returns downstairs he is smiling, resigned to facing whatever tension and arguments the evening will bring.

Two days later Emma sits in a semicircle with the twelve other women who come here every week. The chairs are sturdy and don't have arms, so there is no chance of getting stuck. Emma knows chairs can be a minefield when you're overweight. She always thinks of herself as overweight. Obese is such an ugly word.

Emma looks round the room at the nice, ordinary women: teachers, doctors and housewives who look after children or elderly relatives, are local counsellors, charity workers and who sing in choirs and have not-unhappy marriages. But when it comes to food they are overwhelmed: it is the one area of their life they can't sort out. For them, food has a power they can't explain or, more importantly, resist.

The group leader calls Emma's name and asks her to, *Come behind the screen and stand on the scales please.* Emma has gained two pounds. The group leader refrains from commenting. She just tells

Emma the number and writes it down. Emma thinks the group leader should say something consoling. Emma waits and the group leader knows Emma is waiting and Emma knows the group leader knows. Eventually Emma goes back to her seat. When everyone has been weighed the meeting starts.

While the group leader talks about how to stay motivated, Emma ponders why the group leader is three, maybe four stones overweight. A voice in Emma's head asks, *Surely, if she follows her own advice she should be slim?* In previous meetings, Emma has pushed this thought aside. Tonight it takes root. When the group leader stops talking Emma puts up her hand: something about these sessions makes her act as if she is back at school.

The group leader listens carefully to Emma's question. As she tries to remain poised, her ample breasts heave and her breath rasps her lips, which, Emma notices, are the only thin aspect of her. One of the other women says, *Sorry, I didn't hear what was asked,* so the group leader repeats it. Her voice is higher-pitched than usual. Her face, double chin and neck are scarlet.

The women sitting in the semicircle stare at Emma then quickly return their attention to the group leader. This is the million-dollar question not one of them has been brave enough to ask. The silence becomes awkward, uncomfortable. Some of the women feel their hearts racing, some start to sweat, but still no one speaks.

With a suppressed sob ricocheting through her voice, the group leader explains, *These weekly sessions are about your weight, not mine. This is your time to focus on understanding and improving your relationship with food. However, in answer to the question, being this weight is a choice I've made because... well... err... because... um...* Seeing the hurt in the group leader's eyes, Emma wishes she had never asked.

Bitch. Bitch. Bitch. Bitch, Fiona, the group leader, yells in her head as she tries to stay poised and keep smiling. She tells herself, *I will not cry in front of these women. I absolutely will not cry.* What happens next is a blur of tears and apologies.

After the meeting, Fiona drives to a neighbouring town and joins the queue at Ray's Plaice. When she gets to the counter she orders, *A large cod and four large portions of cheesy chips.* She explains, *My husband and sons don't like fish, so I'm just getting them chips.* She always feels the need to explain when she buys fast-food, chocolate or sweets. The man serving shrugs.

Fiona sees her deception reflected in the man's eyes. His look says as loudly as if he had spoken, *You don't have a husband or any sons. You're going to eat all this yourself. If I had a pound for every fat woman who claimed to be buying chips for someone else I would be living in Acapulco.* Fiona pays and flees to her car. As she drives, her parcel of food is warm in her lap – warm and comforting. She parks behind some recycling bins and cries as she unwraps the paper.

Fiona bites into the batter... swallows almost immediately... bites in again... fills her mouth with cheese and chips... eats more batter... eats more cheese and chips... She catches sight of herself in the rear-view mirror and nods as her reflection says, *Food really can be a comfort. It can soothe the bruise left by an insult. It can ease a broken heart. You lie when you tell your clients anything different.* Fiona sits in the car nodding and eating and every greasy mouthful makes her feel better.

Halfway through the second portion of cheesy chips Fiona starts to smile. Every week, she tells women sitting in a semicircle not to eat unless they have true, physical hunger. When they ask how they will know, she tells them to drink a glass or two of water then wait ten minutes. If it isn't thirst they are feeling she tells them to check for emotional hunger. To do this, they should spend some time writing down how they feel. Is anger or resentment making them reach for carrot cake? Are they turning to pizza for consolation or to a Danish pastry for solace?

Only when they are sure they have true, physical hunger should they eat healthy food in sensible portions. Fiona looks at her own delicious, fat-laden choice then at her reflection who muses, *It's complex this being overweight business.*

And it is a business. Fiona makes a good living helping other women try to lose weight. She does get some men but it is mostly women. Speaking between bites of batter and cheesy chips, her reflection says, *Their stories are all the same. They diet, lose weight then at a buffet crisps call their name. At lunch with a friend, they spread butter on a roll. They start to have biscuits with their morning coffee. Stressed, they order a takeaway. Insidiously, inevitably, the weight creeps back. Now they eat to soothe their frustration, disbelief, despair.*

Soon they weigh more than they did at the start of the diet. When they look in the mirror they hate themselves. Fiona looks away and fills her mouth with chips and cheese. She keeps pushing in chips until she feels better. She has two more mouthfuls just to be sure then she looks back at her reflection.

Speaking with her mouth full, Fiona's reflection continues, *Then they hear about a new diet and think this might finally be the one. They pay and get on the rollercoaster again.* Fiona's reflection stares accusingly. Fiona feels sick: just-been-on-a-rollercoaster-after-eating jellied-eels sick. She fills her mouth with more cheesy chips in an effort to quell the nausea.

Fiona suspects she is addicted to food but that isn't a word she likes. Addicts hang about in alleys and filthy bedsits. They inject themselves with drugs and steal to fund their habits. *What's wrong with eating food I enjoy and being the size I am if I'm happy?* she asks. Her reflection gives her a look of disbelief then turns away. Fiona feels a sob rising in her throat and buries it in an avalanche of chips and batter.

Stella leaves the group meeting frustrated that Fiona did not have a more convincing answer to Emma's question. As she walks, Stella mutters to herself, *This always happens with diets. I set off following the rules and my weight drops. I feel triumphant, elated. I revel in the compliments and my self-esteem soars. I'm sure I'm going to reach my target weight but something always goes wrong. I really thought Fiona was different. I really thought Fiona was going to help me achieve my dream.*

Stella is convinced her life will be transformed once she can wear a size twelve. She crosses the road muttering, *Then I won't hate myself anymore. I won't envy women walking down the street looking happy and confident because I'll be one of them. Look at me in my size twelve clothes my sexy walk will say. Look at me. Look at me.*

But every time Stella imagines herself walking sexily she feels worried. She has lived her whole adult life cocooned in fat. She reminds herself, *It's the reason my mother has no respect for me, the reason my husband left me, the reason I never get promoted at work, the reason I find it hard to make friends, the reason people talk about me behind my back, the reason...* her list goes on and on. *So once I'm slim what will I blame if things don't go as planned?*

I stop writing, put down my pen and stare out the window. *What will Stella blame?* I ask the thrush I can hear singing through the open window. The thrush stops singing and tilts his head, so I read him my last paragraph and confess, *There is something about what I've written that fails to convey the darkness of Stella's fear: the terror, the falling down a mineshaft, the panic that tastes like petrol.* The thrush acknowledges this with a few, repeated, flute-like notes then flies away.

I decide to take a break. I tell myself, *I'll walk round the park for twenty minutes to get some exercise and clear my head.* But there is an autumn chill in the suburban air and looking at the clouds it could easily rain. I put on my shoes then take them off.

I stand barefoot in the hall thinking about all the women in the world who have ever tried to lose weight. I see them in their millions. I see millions of before and after photographs pinned to an endless beige wall, like names on a war memorial.

The women stand awkwardly in size XXL clothes or sit on a beach scoffing ice cream: photographs they would rather forget. Once they have lost weight they smile fit to burst, ride a bike, dance salsa, stand in one leg of old trousers - anything to show how wonderful their life is now. They see a slender future.

I wave and shout, *Don't be so smug, so naive. In six months, most of you will have regained weight, often much more than you lost.* But they can't or don't want to hear my warning. They continue smiling proudly, like my grandfather, in the only photograph I have of him. I wander over to the piano and pick up the photograph.

He is standing by his homemade, newly-varnished boat. At a guess, he weighs eleven stone. It is the fattest he will ever be. He is waving, before rowing into sun and cherry blossom, down the Volga towards Stalingrad and ten years hard labour, because the neighbour who took the photograph was arrested and could not hold out. Beaten, sleep deprived, not fed for days, the neighbour wrote down my grandfather's name in return for a bowlful of cabbage soup and half a salted herring.

My grandfather did not bear a grudge. If the subject came up, he would gently deflect it. He would suggest that until I had sat in that windowless room, beaten and hungry and afraid for my life, I had no idea what decisions I would make. Then he would quote Walt Whitman, 'I find no sweeter fat than sticks to my own bones.'

I make myself go back to my desk.

By late afternoon, I am still unable to find the right words to convey Stella's fear. I tell myself, *I hate you for failing. A brief description that really caught the fear's essence would have made a brilliant ending.* I thump my forehead with the palm of my hand and chide, *You're stupid. You're stupid.* If anyone else spoke to me like this I would be livid, but I take it as truth from myself.

I wander round the house and end up standing in the kitchen with a cupboard door open. I take out the bag of doughnuts I bought this morning.

I bite through crisp, fried dough. Raspberry jam oozes, drips like blood onto my arm. Sugar sticks to my lips. I finish one doughnut then start another. There are four more doughnuts in the bag. I count them twice, just to be sure. I start to feel calm. I bite into a third doughnut and, as I chew, I tell myself, *Finding the right ending to my story doesn't matter. Until these doughnuts are finished, the ending can wait.*

Emma Sharp is 37 and lives in Great Dunmow, Essex, with her husband and two young children. A qualified accountant originally from Harlow she is currently working on her first novel.

<u>Diary of an Essex Girl</u>

Monday 21st August 1989

It was my birthday yesterday. 11 years old. I got a Cabbage Patch Doll. I kept telling Mum which one I wanted but she just nodded and didn't say anything so I thought she wasn't listening. Mum and Dad took us to Clacton for the day. It was brilliant. We went to the funfair and then went paddling in the sea. We all got ice cream at the end and Tony was sick in the car on the way home. Erghh! I'm sure Jess's brother, David, isn't as disgusting as mine. David is really tall and is always nice to me. He looks like Matt Goss. He is fourteen the same age as my brother. Tony is tall too but skinny and has loads of disgusting spots all over his ugly face. He always teases me for being a little girl but I'm going to secondary school in two weeks and then he won't be able to any more.

Jess came over today and I showed her my new doll. I think she was really jealous. She hasn't got a Cabbage Patch Doll. Her mum just got her a Barbie for her birthday. We can't wait to go to secondary school. We are just praying we will be put in the same class. We are the only two children going from our school so if we're not together we won't know anyone at all.

I heard Mum and Dad shouting at each other last night when I was in bed. I couldn't hear what they were saying but then I heard Mum coming up the stairs and the front door slamming downstairs. I thought I could hear Mum crying in her room. I was going to see if she was OK but I was worried she might tell me off for not being asleep.

Monday 4th September 1989

I start school tomorrow! Really excited but nervous too. Fingers crossed me and Jess are together. I've got all my uniform

hanging up on my wardrobe ready. We
have to wear a blazer with the school
logo on and a navy blue pleated skirt. I
never had to wear a uniform before so it
feels really weird when I try it on. Me
and Mum went out the other day and
bought all my stationery because you
have to take your own and a new
rucksack to carry everything in. I even
have to have a calculator!

Tuesday 5th September 1989

Me and Jess are together yippee! We
don't get to sit next to each other in class
though as we have to be in alphabetical
order and my name's Fields and she's
Porter. I'm sitting next to Graham
Edwards on one side and Stacy Foster on
the other. Stacy has her ears pierced and
I'm sure she was wearing make-up. She's
quite nice though. Me, her and Jess
stayed together during break time when
we went out into the playground. I saw
Tony out there but he ignored me which

is fine by me. I don't want everyone to know that my brother is Mr Acne 1989.

Dad was home for dinner for a change but didn't even ask me how my first day had been. He didn't speak to Mum either. The only thing he said was to tell Tony to take his elbows off the table. Then he just finished his dinner, went upstairs, had a bath and went out. He didn't even come and say goodnight to me before he went. Mum said Dad is just really tired from working so hard at work.

Sunday 1st April 1990

Mum and Dad had another row. They usually don't row in front of us but they did today. Mum sent us up to our rooms right in the middle of Beadle's About. I sneaked into Tony's room to see if he knew what they were going on about. Tony said Dad had cheated on Mum. I don't know what that means but I didn't want to ask him as he would just take the mickey out of me. I will ask Stacy tomorrow at school. She knows everything. We heard the front door slam and crept downstairs. Mum was crying on the stairs but tried to hide it when she heard us coming. I asked if she was alright but she just hugged me and then went into the kitchen and carried on washing up.

Monday 2nd April 1990

Stacy said that cheating means having sex with someone who you are not married to. I don't know exactly what sex is but I think it means Dad has been kissing another lady other than my mum. No wonder she is always crying. When I get married I hope my husband doesn't kiss other ladies.

Friday 20th April 1990

Dad is moving out. He came up to my room and told me when he got home from work. He didn't say why, just that he and Mum still loved me and I would still see him all the time. He said he is going to stay at Uncle David's but I know that they only have two bedrooms so I don't know where he is going to sleep. He gave me a big hug and when I looked up at him I think he was crying.

Sunday 22nd April 1990

Nan and Grandad took us to Alton Towers yesterday. It was amazing! I went on all the scary rides even one which Tony was too scared to go on. Grandad came on it with me and his glasses flew off when we went upside down. It was really funny. He had to get one of the men that works there to find them for him. We are staying at their house again tonight and Grandad is going to drive us to school in the morning.

Monday 23rd April 1990

All Dad's stuff has gone from the bathroom. His toothbrush, razor and talcum powder aren't there anymore. Mum said he is going to pick us up on

Saturday morning and take us out somewhere. Saturday is a long time away. I don't know why I can't see him before then but Mum said I just can't and to stop asking her. She keeps cuddling us all the time and hardly says anything. I think she must really miss Dad. They had been together since she was fourteen so it must be really weird for her not having him around.

Monday 14th May 1990

I've got a front door key!! Mum started her new job today so she said me and Tony have to have keys as she won't be home when we get back from school now. It was so cool! Me and Tony raced to the front door when we got off the bus after school and I beat him and opened the door with my key. He punched me in the arm though which really hurt. He's such a grumpy idiot these days. All he does when he gets home is make himself something to eat and then takes it up to his bedroom and puts on his stupid records. He has got one called Nirvana which is just a load of shouting. Mum doesn't let him play it loud when she's home but this afternoon he had it on top volume. I couldn't even hear Neighbours.

Tuesday 25th December 1990

I can't wait. We are seeing Dad tomorrow. We haven't seen him for ages. We are supposed to see him every over weekend but sometimes he rings Mum on a Friday night and says he can't have us. Mum gets really angry when he does this even though she thinks I can't hear her on the phone. She doesn't realize I stand in the hallway and listen to her talking to him. I heard her call Dad's new girlfriend a bitch once. I had never heard Mum swear before so she really mustn't like her. I don't really like her either but I don't think she's a bitch. She just doesn't know how to talk to children as she doesn't have any. She always talks to me like I'm about 5 even though she's probably not much older than I am.

Mum bought me a make-up doll for Christmas. You can do her hair and make-up and then it rubs off and you can do it all again. It wasn't the Barbie one I wanted though. I think she got it from the market but it's nearly as good as the real thing.

Wednesday 20th March 1991

I just went downstairs to get a glass of water and Mum was sitting at the dining table crying. She had loads of letters all spread out over the table and was writing a long list of numbers onto a bit of paper. When I asked her what was wrong she just smiled and said nothing but I don't know why she won't just tell me. I might be able to help.

Friday 5th April 1991

Tony was supposed to be looking after me tonight but has just gone out with his friends. I told him he wasn't meant to leave me alone as Mum had made him promise to look after me every Thursday and Friday when she goes to her new job at the pub but he just laughed at me. I was going to hit him but Jess's brother, David, was there and I didn't want him to think I was a cow so I just watched as they walked off down the street. I'm sure I saw Tony getting a cigarette out of his pocket. I might tell Mum if he is horrible to me again.

I don't even know why she has to work in the pub when she already works every day at the insurance office. She said we need more money to pay the bills but when I said she should ask Dad she just laughed. I don't know why that's funny. He must have money because he has just been on holiday for two weeks to Gran Canaria with Tanya.

Friday 14th June 1991

Tony is in so much trouble. He was brought home by police tonight. I think he was drunk. He had all sick down the front of his shirt. It was disgusting. They wanted to know where Mum was so when I told them she was working at the pub they made me phone her and get her to come home. She was not happy. By the time she got back Tony was asleep on the sofa. She told me go to bed while she and the policemen sat at the table and talked but I didn't. I sat on the stairs and tried to listen. I could hear them saying that he had been fighting in the town centre and if they caught him again they would have to arrest him. My mum was really upset and kept thanking them for bringing him home and how sorry she was and that we were a good family and that Tony was just struggling to cope with his dad leaving us. I think the policemen were being quite nice but she sounded really worried.

Wednesday 17th July 1991

Major gossip from school today. Sophie Leaman in the fourth year is pregnant and is not coming back to school after the summer holidays!! She's only fifteen. Everyone thinks she's a right slag but Stacy says that she has had sex and it can easily happen. Me and Jess didn't believe her. She's always making stuff like that up although we know that she has snogged Simon Lloyd as we saw her when we went to the pictures for her birthday. I don't think I'll ever have the guts to do anything like that. My dad says that boys only want one thing. I'm not sure exactly what he means but I think he's just trying to say to keep away from them which is fine by me. Except David of course. If he ever asked me out I think I would faint!

Monday 19th August 1991

Mum and Tony had a massive row tonight and he walked out. He was supposed to pick up his GCSE results today from school but he didn't go so Mum went to get them herself. He failed everything apart from an E he got for CDT. When she got home she went ballistic but he just shouted back. She said that he was always out drinking with his friends when he should have been at home revising. He said that she didn't know what she was talking about and that it was nothing to do with her anyway. He even swore at her. He then said that it was his life and he didn't need GCSEs as he was going to form a band and make money that way. I don't know how he is going to be in a band when he can't even play a musical instrument. What an idiot. In the end I heard the door slam and watched as he walked up the path. It's half eleven now and he still hasn't come back. I heard Mum on the phone to Dad asking him to go out and look for him but I don't know if he will or not. He always seems to be busy these days since Tanya got pregnant.

Friday 14th February 1992

Me and Mum are moving on Monday.
Mum said we can't afford the rent here
anymore and have to move to a flat
which means we won't have a garden
anymore. We went to see it a few weeks
ago. It is on the eighth floor of a big
tower block and doesn't even have a
balcony. My room is tiny and I can only
open the window a bit in case I fall out.
You have to get up to your floor in a lift
which smells disgusting. I'm sure
someone has weed in there. Mum says
that we only need two bedrooms now
that Tony has moved out to share a
house with some of his mates and it will
be a lot cheaper there. I don't know why
we can't just stay where we are. I'm sure
Dad would help her pay for it if she
would only ask him for some money.
And it means I won't be able to walk to
Jess's house anymore because it is right
across town. I will have to take my bike
which will take ages.

The only good thing that is happening to me at the moment is that I got a Valentine's Day card in the post this morning. It must be from David as I don't think any of the boys in my class know my address. And they're all ugly anyway so I hope it wasn't from one of them.

Wednesday 19th August 1992

Me and Mum have only just got back from the hospital. Mum was mugged tonight in the stairwell when she got home from work and they punched her in the face and ran off with her shopping and handbag. She is OK but had to have some stitches. She wouldn't stop crying as she said they had taken my birthday present which she had got me for tomorrow. A little gold bracelet it was apparently. She said it wasn't even worth a lot of money but they just took everything. She kept saying sorry to me that I wouldn't have anything to open tomorrow but I'm not worried about that.

I just hate this flat. It's so noisy all the time and there are always horrible people hanging around in the stairwell which doesn't matter so much if the lift is working but it usually isn't. I hope Mum is going to be OK. She was so upset.

Thursday 20th August 1992

I cannot believe what happened tonight! After thinking I was going to have the worst birthday ever it has turned out to be the best. Me, Jess and Stacy went to the cinema together and met David and his friend Richard in the queue outside. We were all going to see the same film so we ended up sitting together and David sat next to me!!!! But that's not the best part. About halfway through the film, he reached over and took my hand. I could hardly breathe. He didn't let go until the credits started. I couldn't even look at him I was so embarrassed. I know he must think I'm such an idiot. Stacy has already lost her virginity and I haven't even kissed anyone yet. I can't even hold hands with a boy without turning to jelly. Except that David's not a boy. He's 17! After the cinema everyone was saying goodbye only I was too scared to say anything to him so I just walked off. I wonder if he really does like me.

Friday 25th December 1992

I can't believe it. David bought me a gold necklace with a little heart pendant on it for Christmas. It's really beautiful and I'm going to wear it for the rest of my life. He gave it to me the other day and told me I mustn't open it until today. I could hardly wait. He kissed me for the first time. Just on the lips, not a real snog, but it was amazing. I don't know if that means he is my boyfriend now. I will have to ask Stacy when I see her. She has gone to stay with her dad for Christmas in Peterborough or somewhere. I can't ask Jess because David is her brother and that would be weird. It would freak me out if anyone started asking me things like that about my brother. Although I don't suppose anyone would want him at the moment. Last time me and Mum went to see him in the rehab centre he looked like a skeleton. His eyes looked massive in his head and he had little red marks all over his arm. Mum keeps saying he will get better soon. She is saving up to move to another flat with another bedroom so he can come back to live with us even though Tony keeps saying he doesn't want to come back home. I said that he could have my bedroom and I would sleep on the sofa. He grabbed me and hugged me so hard when I said that I could barely breathe.

Friday 20th August 1993

My mum went ballistic when I told her that me and David are going out together. I was so scared to tell her which is why I made David keep it a secret until my fifteenth birthday. I thought it might sound better if I was fifteen already. She said that he is too old for me and was only after one thing and that I would be pregnant before I knew it then my life would be ruined. I cried when she said this because me and David have only kissed and held hands. He says he loves me and will wait until I'm ready. I can't believe Mum would think like that about me. She made me promise that I wouldn't do anything until I'm 18 which I did just to shut her up.

Thursday 18th August 1994

I got my GCSE results today! I got six As and three Bs. I'm so happy. It means I can do the A Levels I want to at college. I'm going to do English Language, French and Geography. Just think if I get my A Levels I'll be able to get a really good job. David is training to be a mechanic so one day we should have enough money for a decent flat and get out of this hell-hole. Maybe Mum will be able to save more now I'm giving her some housekeeping from my job at the shoe shop and she might be able to move one day too. She still thinks that Tony will come back one day even though he moved out of the rehab centre and has his own room in a shared house. They are all addicts at his house though which seems a bit stupid as I'm sure they will all encourage each other.

Friday 23rd August 1996

I can't believe it's nearly here. David and I are getting married tomorrow! I am so excited. I just wish that Tony was well enough to come. He didn't even recognize me when I went to see him last week. And Dad just said he can't make it. He didn't even give a reason. At least it's only at the Registry Office so I don't need anyone to walk me down the aisle.

Mum was not at all pleased when we first told her. She said that I am way too young and could go to university if I wanted to and then get married later on. I tried to explain to her that I can't afford to go to university because she and Dad earn too much for me to get a grant. The fact that Dad hasn't given me a penny since he moved out is clearly irrelevant to the grants people. Anyway David and I were going to save to buy our own place. She just kept saying that I didn't know what I was doing and that I would end up like her. The thing is I know that she's wrong. I just know that things will be different for us. Why wouldn't they?

Jim Reeve was brought up in the East End of London , left home at fifteen, did his National Service in the RAF Regiment and then joined the Met Police for a period, after which he worked for the Greater London Council as a housing officer in Bethnal Green. He concluded his housing career as a District Manager of the largest housing area with Basildon Development Corporation. His career has given him a depth of experience to draw on for his writing. He is married and has two sons and five wonderful grandchildren and a great-granddaughter.

He has had six non-fiction books and a number of short stories published in magazines.   He has won, and been placed in a number of local and national competitions, including RAC, Society of Women Writers and Journalists, Writer of the Year for Basildon and Writer's Magazine, Age Concern, plus the Jack Kendal Trophy three times and the Meggs Cup. He has written three novels, two plays and two comedies. He loves writing fiction, having started his writing career by writing under the bed covers with a torch after being forbidden to do so by his very strict step-father He now writes in his summer house, named the Mouse House. He is the Treasurer of Brentwood Writer's Circle.

 His web-site is www.jim-reeve.com

It's a Kind of Magic

How could an ordinary brown suitcase have changed one's existence?

How could it have turned one's life on its head leading to a lie of happiness and contentment. It is difficult to believe that a suitcase has such powers but mine has!

As I carefully packed my Royal Air Force kitbag to go on an exercise, I knew that, no matter how carefully I put my clothes in, they would come out like rags and I hated ironing. I decided it was time to do something about it.

After the exercise, I visited the village shop in Fassberg Germany, where I was doing National Service and bought a brown suit case for 12 marks, which was about a pound in 1956.

A few days later, my anticipation began to grow as I put my application in for U.K. leave, with the added bonus of avoiding crumpled clothes and no ironing. Then one of my squad cast his envious eye on my case and asked if he could borrow it to go on leave. He promised he would be back long before I was due to go. Despite grave misgivings I finally gave in. I should have known better; he was renowned for being unreliable. He returned, minus my case!

The air was blue! It was only the fear of having my leave cancelled that we did not come to blows but I was determined to recover my case. After some friendly persuasion I extracted his address and was pleased to find his parents lived near mine. A fortnight later, with my clothes crammed into my kitbag I left for the UK.

Towards the end of my three weeks I decided it was time to recover my case, and so I visited his parents. In camp, this colleague was always boasting about his large house and how affluent his parents were. As I turned the corner into his street I expected to see a palace or at least a castle but there, stretching out before me, was a row of ordinary two-up and two-down terrace houses. His middle aged parents were charming and after handing back my precious case invited me back for tea the following Sunday and being broke and with nothing else to do, I accepted.

A week later, I turned up, feeling confident and wanting to impress his parents I wore my best uniform, displaying my senior air force badge and crossed rifles. As they opened the door I thought I had arrived at a young man's heaven, for there, standing by the side of his parents was this beautiful angel. I could hear my heart thumping. I was having difficulty breathing. My voice croaked. I was so taken with her I did not even hear her name as we were introduced but I could see by the sparkle in her eyes the feeling was mutual. The afternoon went in a magical blur as we had tea, gazing into each other's eyes. Later she sat on the floor at my feet while we listened to Top Twenty on Radio Luxemburg. Occasionally, she would glance back with her big brown eyes and smile, sending quivers of desire through my body.

Suddenly, as in Cinderella, the clock struck twelve but luckily her dress did not turn into rags nor did she lose a glass slipper but it was time to go. Soon we were in the street and the door closed behind us. Perhaps my colleague had been right and he did live in a magic castle after all and I had just met its princess. I put my arm around her to guide her across the road and in an instant we were kissing, spot lighted by the harvest moon.

We finally reached the bus stop only to find that the last bus had gone, so we walked in a haze to Leytonstone Station, stopping occasionally to embrace, only to find when we got there that the last train had gone. We telephoned her parents from the box outside the station. It was still there up to ten years ago and we always smiled when we saw it, remembering our first few hours. Her mother was frantic. " Don't move, I'll send a taxi." As the taxi drew up I felt in my pocket to ensure I had enough money for the fare, luckily I had. I was warmly greeted by her mother and father and was treated to one of her mother's famous cheese and tomato sandwiches which melted in the mouth. At two o'clock in the morning I sat at the kitchen table before a roaring fire, talking to her father,who had been in the Royal Flying Corps during the First World War and was a retired rubber planter. As we talked the door opened and one by one Anne's five brothers and sisters poked their heads round it to inspect me.

The final straw came when an old, bent lady, with a wart on her face, put her head round the door. Apparently, my future mother-in-law had taken her in many years before, as a domestic help as she had nowhere to go.

Next morning, I travelled up to London with Anne and after drawing out the last of my savings, waited around until lunchtime when I took her to Lyons Corner House for lunch. To impress her, I asked if she wanted wine, praying she would say "No" as I could not afford it. I remember we had braised beef, carrots and mashed potatoes served by a waitress in a black and white uniform with a little cap on her head. In the evening we travelled back to Anne's house, having been invited by her parents to stay the night. Although the bus was crowded, as far as we were concerned, we only had eyes for each other. I remember the conductor saying

"Isn't love grand!"

I had only three days left and we spent them in a love mist. Finally, it was time to go back and I had to catch the 9pm train from Liverpool Street

Station to Harwich for the troop ferry. We sat in the station for as long as we dared, after all, I would not see her for five months, when I was due for demob. Reluctantly, we parted and I watched her off but I had left it too long, I had missed the train! Not sure what to do, I reported to the transport sergeant who shrugged his shoulders as if it was an everyday occurrence, which to him it probably was but to me I knew I was in trouble, I was absent without leave. He instructed me to report to Whitehall the next morning, which I did and was told to come back in two days' time as there was not another military train until then. Pretending I was in Germany, I telephoned Anne and asked "Would you like to go out to lunch?" She giggled, pleased to hear from me and whispered down the telephone "I'd love to but it's a bit far to travel just for lunch!"

"Would two days be enough then?"

"If only! It's a long way!"

"I have magic powers, see you in five minutes." We went to Lyons again. Then we had two extra wild exciting days in which we talked and talked, walked hand in hand through Hyde Park and got to know each other so that after my extended leave we decided to get engaged when I got demobbed.

All good things have to end and so after two days extra leave, Anne stood on the platform waving me good-bye. With a heavy heart I leaned out of the carriage window and watched her disappear into the distance. Suddenly, the carriage door was thrown open, tumbling me out of my dream world as a Red Cap glared down at me and demanded my pass. As he stared at it, my heart stopped while I waited for him to discover I had been absent without leave. Suddenly he looked up, his face breaking into a sarcastic grin. "You're late, Airman and I'm charging you!"

I swallowed hard and looking him straight in the eyes I replied "I've already been charged at Whitehall, Corporal." Disappointed, he returned my papers. All the way back to camp, each time I was challenged I told the same story, "I've already been charged at Whitehall!"

As I stood outside the guardroom at Fassberg, the Air Force Police Sergeant glared down at me.

"You're late!"

I repeated my story and he marked their records "Awaiting Charge."

They are still waiting to this day!

For five months Anne and I wrote to each other each day. I had just crossed the last day off my demob calendar and was lying back on my bed anticipating our meeting and listening to the radio when my world was shattered. The announcer said sternly "British Forces have invaded the Suez

Canal." Being a signaller I knew there was a good chance they would send me and cancel my demob. Fassberg was an enormous airfield and it took two days to visit every department to obtain a signature to say you had returned any equipment you had borrowed. Every moment of those 48 hours I dreaded to hear that my demob had been cancelled.

When I finally walked out of the gate at R.A.F. Cardington in England, I breathed a sigh of relief, I was free! I got home and asked Anne's father if I could marry her, as was the tradition in those days.

We married the following year and took the brown case on honeymoon packed neatly with our clothes. That was fifty three years ago this September and the old brown case is now a bit battered but is still working its magic as it sits in the attic. In it is my neatly folded R.A.F uniform.

Karen Bowman was born in London and has lived in Essex since she was 10 years old. A social historian, she has long worked as a freelance writer and is a popular public speaker. She is a member of the Society of Woman Writers & Journalists and the Historical Writers Association. Her books include: *Essex Girls, Essex Boys and Corsets & Codpieces, A Social History of Outrageous Fashion.* The piece that follows, while it makes a self-contained entry, is an extract from her first book *Essex Girls.*

ELIZABETH I – A LADY OF 'PROGRESS'
(1533-1603)

'When it pleaseth her in the summer season to recreate herself abroad, and view the state of the country, every nobleman's house is her palace...' (from William Harrison's 'Description of England')

What constitutes an Essex Girl? For our purposes it's not necessarily just the accident of birth. Perhaps not born in Essex, Queen Elizabeth I did spend much of her childhood in the county, in Havering-atte-Bower, a palace which later became the starting off or finishing point for many of her travels. During her captivity as a young princess she had also lived in many Essex country houses, her nomadic lifestyle with spells in the tower teaching her just how fickle public opinion could be. It was a lesson well learned for, once Queen Elizabeth decided that England's prosperity and thus her power would be based upon the love and devotion of her people, she was determined to make royal popularity the cornerstone of her reign.

The great Elizabethan 'Progress' was the mechanics behind this life time public relations exercise. Every spring and summer of her 44 year reign she made sure she was seen by and moved among her people, even if the contrast between their lifestyles and hers were quite incompatible. In doing so, she successfully made her subjects her greatest asset. They in turn could see for themselves what a great Queen she was.

And what was she like, the Virgin Queen? We have the French Ambassador's report to the French king in 1595, when her half-sister Queen Mary still occupied the throne: 'She is tall with a good skin... she has fine eyes and above all, beautiful hands... Her intellect and understanding are wonderful... Proud and haughty, as although she knows she was born of such a mother, she nevertheless does not consider herself of inferior in degree to the Queen, whom she equals in self-esteem; nor does she believe herself less legitimate than her Majesty, alleging in her own favour that her mother would never cohabit with the King unless by way of marriage, with the authority of the Church.... She prides herself on her father and glories in him; everybody saying that she also resembles him more than the Queen does and he therefore always liked her and had her brought up in the same way as the Queen…'

An Englishman's home may have been his castle, but not exclusively. All manors in the land ultimately belonged to the Sovereign, an ancient feudal right which meant she could occupy the house of any subject anywhere at any time. For many this was a chance to impress, an honour to be savoured, a boost for local pride, even if the expenses incurred might cripple the host. There was no redress for being brought near to ruin by the Queen's 'progress', for however difficult or tedious such a journey, there was no compromise on comfort; much of her furniture and even the royal bed had to be carted along.

As Elizabeth seldom set foot more than 20 miles outside of London, these summer forays into the English countryside were also a chance to escape the stifling heat, smells and outbreaks of plague in the city – London theatres closed during these months for just that reason. She would lodge with nobles and gentry in her bid to be seen by many and to win people's hearts ...not to mention the considerable saving on royal household expenses.

Elizabeth made in excess of four hundred visits to individual and civic hosts. Towns were obliged and honoured to welcome her, too, between 1558 and 1603. Entertaining the Queen could not be avoided.

While Essex has no unique claim on Elizabeth, it was a well-favoured destination. In Essex the Queen visited the ancient boroughs of Maldon, Colchester, Harwich and Saffron Walden. She was entertained by Sir William Petre of Ingatestone Hall, by Sir Thomas Mildmay at Moulsham (Sir Thomas is recorded as having complained of the expense), Chelmsford and Lord Darcy at St Osyth. Other great houses were visited at Epping, Great Hallingbury, Ongar, Kelvedon, Gosfield and Abbess Roothing. At Horham Hall, Thaxted, she stayed for as long as nine days...

Elizabeth did not travel light. As she insisted the decor and ambiance of the royal palaces at Greenwich, Whitehall, Richmond and Hampton Court be recreated in the halls and dining rooms of her hosts, so all her furniture, wall hangings, books, pictures, jewels, bedlinen including the royal bed had to be moved in with her. A baggage train of at least three to four hundred carts was needed, the whole entourage spanning on average a distance of ten miles from the first wagon to the last, surely an excursion to be noticed. If lucky, her hosts would be told of her forthcoming visit months in advance and were able to vacate their homes, leaving only an empty shell for the Queen and her court to occupy. If notice was less generous, or the venue a brief stay with minor gentry 'en route' then it was a wise host who made himself scarce and let the 'officers of the chamber' take over the premises lock, stock and barrel.

Elizabeth had the final say with regard to her progresses, but the planning was left to the Privy Council, and the Lord Chamberlain. His responsibility was to the Queen and the accommodation of her immediate attendants, which left the rest of the royal entourage to fend for themselves. Lodging houses in the vicinity of the royal progress were rapidly taken (a chance for the owners to inflate prices and line their own pockets) and when those had been snapped up, tents were put up in the fields and meadows all around – like a miniature Tudor Woodstock.

While the logistics of travel were one aspect to be organized by the Queen's entourage, subsistence fell to the host. Kitchens and cellars needed to be stocked in the manner to which the royal visitor was accustomed. Ingatestone, the brick-built residence of Sir William Petre was one of the stops in the summer of 1561, during a 'progress' that had begun on 14 July at Wanstead House, held by the Earl of Leicester.

Elizabeth arrived at Ingatestone Hall on Friday 19 July and stayed for five days. Sir William was a Devon man with a double degree in canon and civil law at Oxford, who had risen to become a deputy of Thomas Cromwell under the Queen's father. He had served each sovereign since as Principal Secretary – Edward VI and Mary Tudor. He has been described as a 'new man', someone who bent, rather than broke, however the wind blew, in fact the Dictionary of National Biography describes him as being 'sprung from the willow rather than the oak'. He was now one of this

Queen's Principal Secretaries, a senior royal servant and a man of substance, owning 20,000 acres in Essex alone. Obviously his hospitality needed to match his position and his Account Book meticulously listed the expenses incurred. This included Lady Petre's purchase of '13 ells of green taffeta sarcenet' for lining curtains and a quarter lb.of 'fusses', perhaps a Tudor pot pourri for perfuming the royal chambers. What could not be provided from the rabbit-warrens, dovecots, fishponds and store rooms of the tenants on his estate, had to be bought and transported from London.

'A Declarac[i]on of all suche p[ro]vision of victualls and other nessesaries as was bought and p[ro]vided against the quenes Ma[jes]tes com[m]inge to my M[aste]rs howse at yngatstone beinge the xixth day of Julye the thirde yere of her Ma[jes]tes Reigne and there tar[y]inge untill the xxijth of the same both daies included…'

Some of the provisions on that list may interest today's housewives, chefs, as well as naturalists, etc. Besides all the 'white wheate', 'brede', 'beare & ale', there are 'Sea fishe' such as soles, flounders, 'gurnardes', congers and 'sturgion'. Perhaps more surprising are six 'signettes' (young swans), plus four 'signettes' and six 'bitters' from Cambridge, six dozen 'pewettes', a dozen gulls, two dozen 'brewes' (a kind of snipe, a medium sized wading bird), two dozen 'egrettes', twelve dozen 'quailes' from London, equally twelve herons and twelve 'shoulvlers' (spoonbill ducks), plus another eighteen herons and twelve 'shoulvlers' from Kent. Added to that were sums for presents, apart from the dozen capons and two dozen 'chekins' for Sir William's own table…

How the Petre's felt about the hole in their pocket left by their sovereign's visit is not known. But by 5 August Elizabeth had left Ingatestone, in her cumbersome and springless coach, and arrived at Ipswich, the furthermost point of that 'progress'. They had followed a circular route on the great eastern road and thence through northern Essex by way of Hedingham, Leez [Leighs} Priory, her visit with Lord Rich costing him £389, Great Hallingbury and on into Hertford.

It was not always a pleasure for her hosts, nor was it unheard of for nobles to absent themselves from Court in order to avoid being visited. It was not unusual to suffer financial ruin following such an event. You could not slight the Queen by being frugal with your provisions, but making her too welcome might backfire as well, as with Sir John Cutte of Horham Hall near Thaxted. So impressed was the Queen with Sir John's hospitality on her two visits, one which had lasted nine days in 1571, the other for six days in 1578, that she subsequently sent the Spanish Ambassador with his numerous attendants to stay at Horham Hall during an outbreak of plague in London. Alas, Sir John could not afford the extra expense and eventually had to sell off Horham, moving near to Cambridge.

Providence occasionally smiled upon a prospective host, a case in point being Lord Darcy of St Osyth, but not before preparations had been made. The Queen arriving on 30th July 1561 encountered a 'great thunder and lightning as any man had ever heard till past 10, then great rain till midnight.' Causing alarm and panic that 'the people thought the world was at an end, and the day of doom come,' the Queen decided she should move on straight away!

Naturally, the business of state could not be neglected during the Queen's absence, so the Council accompanied her as part of the Court routine, conducting its business wherever she stayed. Special arrangements might have to be implemented to receive and dispatch their reports and instructions. During the Queen's Audley End stay in July 1578 the Council convened at nine meetings. Lord Burleigh was present, the Scottish Ambassador had talks and foreign courtiers were received.

While her Lord Chamberlain and Vice-Chamberlain were responsible for detailed preparation and management, the 'harbingers' travelled ahead to look for suitable lodgings. The plague was the great curse of the time and Mayors of towns and Lords-Lieutenants of counties had to confirm its absence when the Queen's 'gestes' or itineraries were published and their area was favoured. Stocks of fuel, food and of course fodder for the horses had to be provided by towns and villages along the way, a necessity for which a Yeoman Purveyor and a deputy were assigned a Royal Commission ' to take up and provide for us'.

Elaborate preparations might have to be made when a town received notice of the Queen's intended visit. If notice was generous enough, there might be time to spruce up the town and have every house newly painted, including the market cross. Stocks, pillory and cage, normally used to punish malefactors, might have to be removed.

The roads might be rutted and potholed and as they tended to be the responsibility of the parish through which they ran, persuasion and pressure might have to be brought to bear. Even so, streets were strewn with rushes or gravel, muck- hills and middens would be removed so as not to offend her majesty and herbs might disguise troublesome odours. Cows were forbidden into town during the time of a visit.

Flags flew and *'suche lyke, every howse adorned with green boughs…'* Bells rang out at her passing. According to the Chelmsford Churchwarden's Accounts 6s.8d. was paid to the ringers when the Queen came through the town.

Entry into a town would be a great ceremonial occasion. With townsfolk cheering, the Queen was received by bailiff and burgesses and she politely listened to speeches by town recorders. Gifts would be offered and though she professed she came for 'the hearts and allegiance of her subjects' she nevertheless accepted them gracefully. Gifts to the Queen expressed loyalty and affection. At Audley End in July 1578 after being entertained by officials and students from nearby Cambridge University she was presented with a particular favourite, a pair of scented gloves. Opening the gift 'hir Majestie beholding the beautie of the said gloves, as in great admiration, and in token of hir thankfull acceptation of the same, held up one of her hands; and then, smelling into them, putt them half waie upon hir hands.'

During the 'summer progress' of 1561 Elizabeth visited Dovercourt and Harwich. Silas Taylor, Storekeeper at the Naval Yard, writing almost a century later reported on the Queen's visit: 'August 12, 1561, Queen Elizabeth came hither and accepted of an Entertainment from the Borough, lodging, as it is said, for several days at a House about the middle of the High-Street, and being attended by the Magistrates at her Departure as far as the Windmill out of Town, she graciously demanded of them, what they had to request of her, from whom she received this Answer, Nothing, but to wish her Majesty a good journey: Upon which she turned her Horse about, and looking upon the Town said, *A pretty Town and wants nothing,* and so bad them farewel.' (From Samuel Dale in his 'History', a second edition of which appeared in 1732.)

Later Queen Elizabeth's 'sea-hawks' Frobisher, Hawkins, and Drake would set sail on various expeditions from this north Essex harbour, Hawkins himself commanding a small flotilla of the 'the queenes shippes,' out of Harwich in 1588, to engage the Spanish Armada.

Elizabeth's best known visit to Essex was to Tilbury at the anticipation of that very Armada. In May 1588 the Spanish had been sighted off Cornwall and were subsequently defeated and scattered off Gravelines. On 9 August Elizabeth I famously addressed her troops at Tilbury. Every schoolboy knows her proud and rousing words: '…and therefore I am come amongst you all, to lay down my life for my God and for my kingdom and for my people, my honour, and my blood, even in the dust. I know I have the body of a weak and feeble woman, but I have the heart and stomach of a king, and of a king of England too…'

Dr. Leonel Sharp had good reason to remember the day the Queen rode 'as armed Pallas, attended by noble footmen, Leicester, Essex, and Norris, then Lord Marshall, and divers other great lords…' Some time after 1623 Dr. Sharp recalled the Queen's words in a letter to the Duke of Buckingham, presumably accurately, because he'd had to repeat her oration to the troops the following day – after her departure – to ensure they were heard by everyone.

Elizabeth's rousing speech had certainly swelled the hearts of her troops, but equally left the churchwardens of West Tilbury with a bill for damage done by so large a body of men called to arms. Accused by the archdeacon of neglecting their church wall and furniture, the churchwardens replied, *'that church stooles and walls is muche broken downe by means of the campe that did lie there,'* adding that *'there were non at Tilbury campe but Rogues and Rascals'* For such remarks aimed at the queen's patriots, the churchwardens were ordered to repair the damage done at their own expense!

A charming conversation with the wife of her godson Sir John Harrington has been recorded, reflecting the depth of the Queen's belief in the love of her subjects. It is also a poignant reminder that Elizabeth's royal life conflicted on so many levels with that of her own personal happiness. When asking the young woman how she kept the love of her husband, the woman replied, by dealing with him gently, not denigrating him or crossing him so he was assured of her love for him. The Queen likened herself to a wife in her marriage with the people when she replied, '…go to, go to, mistress. You are wisely bent, I find; after such sort do I keep the good-will of my husbands, my good people; for if they did not rest assured of some special love towards them, they would not readily yield me such good obedience.'

Peter Norman was born just after the war in Lancashire, but has lived most of his life in the Thames Corridor in Essex. He spent 30 years serving with Essex Police, most of which was at Southend on Sea, during which time he wrote a large number of short stories.

On his retirement he had more time to devote to his passion of writing and he joined two writing groups, which he now chairs. He lives in Leigh on Sea and has used his intimate knowledge of the picturesque Leigh Old Town and its environs to add 'flesh to the bones' of his book *Watermelon Man,* which was published recently

Butterflies

The butterfly flapped its wings and with every stroke it rose higher and higher into the air until it was nearly level with Marjorie's eyes. Then, with its wings spread out wide it glided gracefully back down again towards the ground. Over and over it repeated the simple routine and in this peculiar manner the butterfly and the small girl made their way slowly along the tow path of the canal without a care in the world. When it flew upwards, Marjorie walked quickly to keep up with it and when it glided back down again she slowed her pace to maintain the optimum distance behind it: the trick was to be patient and to be close enough to stay in contact but far enough away that it would not be frightened by her presence.

Eventually the butterfly reached a small pocket of wild flowers and drifted down to feed. Marjorie held her breath until it had settled and then with practised ease leaned forwards and cupped her hands around the tiny creature. For a few moments she could feel the anxious fluttering against her palms and then it was still. When she finally opened her hands the butterfly remained perfectly motionless and she was able to study it closely. It was a Red Admiral, and the sun glinted off the incandescent red, yellow and blue gossamer wings; off the strange eye patches on their tips which appeared to return her stare with a lazy indolence.

Finally she blew gently into her hands and the butterfly flew away. This time she allowed it to go unmolested. This was her favourite game and this was her favourite place in which to play it.

The Chelmer and Blackwater Navigation would have been a busy industrial lifeline in past years, but those times had long since passed. Nowadays if one or maybe two boats disturbed the green slime that covered the shallow water it was considered to be a busy day.

Beside the canal the tow path was wide and firm and Marjorie knew every inch of it like the back of her hand; it was her home turf. The only parts she did not love were the bridges. In order to keep the spans to a minimum, the tow path under the bridge had been constricted to a narrow walkway, which must have been barely wide enough for the huge horses to pass along when they were towing the barges. Beneath the bridges the water was black and the vivid imagination of a nine year old girl could populate its inky depths with creatures from her wildest nightmares. To pass the danger she would always press her back to the cold brickwork and scuttle sideways like a demented crab as fast as her shaking legs could carry her. It was only when she emerged onto the wide path beyond that she would release the breath she had been holding for fear of breathing in the stench of the beast from the dark water.

The routine was always the same; once safely past the scary bridge she would gather a handful of pebbles from the edge of the path and hurl them into the water in the shadowy depths and shout at the top of her voice, 'Kill the beast! Kill the beast!'

In the past the beast had never ever called back, but this time a deep voice behind her stopped her in mid hurl. 'Don't wake the Kraken!'

She spun around and saw an untidy pile of cardboard in the corner where the red bricks of the bridge blended into a tangle of nettles and brambles. Marjorie relaxed; she could tell that it was not a talking box, because a thin pair of legs and a pair of ancient and worn brown boots protruded from the bottom of the pile. Further up, through a narrow slit a pair of intense brown eyes peered out at her, at the stone still poised for flight in her hand.

'I said, don't wake the Kraken.'

Marjorie put her hands on her hips. 'What's a Kraken?'

A withered hand slipped out and pulled the uppermost piece of cardboard away and the oldest face Marjorie had ever seen slowly came into view. Its hair was a matted tangle of white and grey, its skin, partially concealed behind a rough nicotine stained beard, was like a map of the London Underground engraved into leather, but the smile was warm enough, despite the colour of the teeth it displayed and the gaps between them.

'The Kraken. You don't want to know about the Kraken.'

'Yes I do. Why shouldn't I wake it up?'

'Cause it would rise up from the black water, covered all over in green slime, and gobble you up for disturbing it's sleep.'

Marjorie laughed. 'You're making that up.'

The old man grinned and a soft cackle slipped past his lips, closely followed by a deep rumbling cough which seemed to rise from the pit of his stomach in ever increasing bursts until his whole emaciated body convulsed with the effort.

Marjorie waited politely until he had finished and said, 'Are you going to die?'

The old man tipped his head to one side.

'Only . . . if you was going to die and turn into a ghost . . . would you come back and haunt this bit of canal so we could be friends? . . . I could teach you how to hunt butterflies.'

The deep belly laugh was followed by another round of hacking cough and when it finally subsided he managed, 'I think I'd prefer to live a little longer . . . if it's all the same with you.'

'But we can still be friends, can't we?'

'If you want, but you can be off with you now; I was asleep and I'm more of a bugger than the Kraken when I'm disturbed.'

Marjorie spotted a small white butterfly and skipped off along the tow path, calling over her shoulder, 'Ok. I'll come back and see you tomorrow . . . if you're not dead.'

For the next few days Marjorie hunted her butterflies as usual, but she made sure she always ended up at the bridge with her new friend. He was raggedy and scruffy and grumpy and he smelt of sweat and stale tobacco and, she had to be completely honest with herself, he also smelt a little bit of wee-wee. However, despite all of those horrid things, when he smiled it was warm and he was kind and gentle and he made her laugh. She had never had a friend quite like him before.

On Monday morning she skipped along the tow path, scuttled crabwise through the bridge, tried hard not to wake the Kraken and peeped around the corner . . .

He was not there. The cardboard was still there, but there were two council men trying to fold it up and stuff it into big black sacks.

She backed behind the bridge, confused, upset.

She heard the younger of the two council men ask, 'D'ya reckon he's died?'

'He might be for all I know. They took him to Broomfield yesterday afternoon. Nights are getting colder. It's not right 'im sleepin' out 'ere like this at 'is age – he ain't no spring chicken.'

Marjorie groaned. No, he certainly was not a spring chicken; she hoped against hope that she was not too late.

She ran up the path, over the embankment and hurried through the empty streets of the industrial estate. She was lucky the hospital was not too far away. As she got to the high, ornate gates she stopped. She had no idea where he would be. She was certain he would not still be in the Emergency Room. She traced her finger across the large colourful map of the departments – he would either be in one of the wards or . . . or in the morgue.

Methodically she worked her way through corridor after corridor until, finally, in Herbert Jeffery Ward she stopped. There he was, in the bed beside the window. She crept across and stood beside his bed. It wasn't the same man she knew – well, she supposed he *was* the same man, but they had washed him up a bit; his hair was clean and combed and he didn't smell of all that stuff anymore. He just looked like someone's granddad.

And, thankfully, he wasn't dead, because she could see his chest rising and falling and could hear his breathing coming out in soft, rasping bursts. He didn't sound very good, but he was still alive. She settled into the high wing-backed chair beside the bed and waited patiently – she didn't want to awaken the Kraken; he said it could be a bugger when it was disturbed.

An hour passed and Marjorie's eyes kept closing; it was so hot and stuffy in here. She was just drifting off when a deep voice said, 'What in tarnation you doin' here?'

She was instantly wide awake. 'They told me you was dead, so I had to see for myself, didn't I?'

The man laughed. 'Well, I'm sorry to disappoint you.'

'I'm not disappointed . . . I just didn't want you to die and your ghost just sort of drift away, like.'

At that moment a lady in a green uniform pushed the tea trolley noisily into the ward and called across, 'Do you want a cup of tea, Harold?'

Harold turned to Marjorie in the high wing-backed chair. 'Would you like some tea, Marjorie?'

The lady in the green uniform looked at the empty chair and asked, 'Who are you talking to, Harold?'

Harold looked at the lady and then at Marjorie in the chair and then back at the lady again. The look on her face told it all . . . she couldn't see the girl.

An intense pain flashed across his chest. He let out a sharp croaking hiss, clutched his heart and dropped back against his pillows. The machine behind his head flat-lined with a harsh scream.

The lady rushed out of the ward shouting for help, but after a few moments Harold sat up and through his ephemeral form Marjorie could clearly see his lifeless body slumped where it had fallen. She slipped her hand into his and squeezed.

'It's ok, Harold, it's just you and me now . . . come on, I'll teach you how to hunt butterflies.'

Dr Philippa Hawley is married with two grown up children and lives in Wivenhoe, where alongside her husband she worked as a GP for 27 years. The Hospice movement has always been close to her heart and she took courses at St Helena Hospice in Colchester before becoming clinical lead in palliative care at the Wivenhoe Surgery.

Since retiring from professional practice Philippa has had time to enjoy walking, gardening, reading and creative writing. She has published two novels; *There's No Sea in Salford*, the story of a Sri Lankan nurse in England, returning home to Sri Lanka after the 2004 Indian Ocean tsunami, and *How They Met Themselves* about a young man's travels in North America. Philippa enjoys travelling with her husband and this, and her previous medical experience, has become a source of inspiration for her writing.

An Essex Walk

Seven miles one way, fourteen there and back – walking from pier to pier and raising money for local cancer charities was to be a treat for eight women and a dog called Alfie. I lived just seventeen miles from Clacton pier but I hadn't trodden on those wooden boards since my children were small. Now in my 50s I returned with my sister and six friends. We were excited, happy to be setting off together, networking, cementing friendships and keeping fit. Alfie would entertain us and make us smile as wagging his metronome tail and pulling on his lead in a private tug of war.

The morning mist was clearing and the air smelt fresh with no hint of that potentially sickly mix of fish and chips with candyfloss so often found at the seaside. Giant gulls hovered over us, squawking in noisy protest, complaining we'd invaded their space, and threatening to drop excrement on our heads. We queued to register our presence and watched the sea roll in beneath the pier's huge nineteenth century frame. Waves wriggled round the wooden support posts and I couldn't believe those stilts, as thick as a man's waist, had lasted so long. I thought Queen Victoria must have been almost my age when the pier was built but she had probably never experienced the freedom to walk that we now enjoyed.

A passing whiff of hot chocolate drifted in the wind over the path and I suddenly travelled back half a century, recalling family visits we'd made to my aunt's house in Essex when we were children growing up in Hertfordshire. Auntie Betty had recently died at the age of 84, having lived and taught for many years in Clacton and my thoughts turned to her as we found our way to the starting line of the organised walk. Our parents had brought my sister, Jane and me to Clacton for summer holidays as little girls in the late 1950s. We stayed with Auntie Betty and Uncle Francis in their sprawling pebble-dashed bungalow set in a lovely orchard, which seemed huge at the time, but probably wasn't. Their home smelt of apples all the year round, a testament to their efficient method of storing them wrapped in paper, in wooden trays in the spare room. We were allowed play with the cat and explore secret corners the furry creature's territory. We would make dens in the bushes, or climb trees to pick our own apples for breakfast; an Essex adventure holiday for two little girls.

We were taken to the beach to paddle, build sandcastles and have donkey rides. I don't remember swimming in the sea but the highlight of the week was always a visit to the pier's outdoor swimming pool. Our mother and her brother, Francis wouldn't join us, but Auntie Betty came along with Dad and Jane and me. Jane and I had those costumes made of material like nylon bubble wrap, that sagged when they got wet. Mine was green. We all wore white rubber swimming caps that hurt your hair when you pulled them on and off. We laughed at our father's hairy chest when he emerged from the men's changing room in his trunks. I don't think men often showed off their chests in those days; at least our dad didn't.

The thing I remembered most clearly was that the water in the pool was freezing; so cold it must have been imported from The Arctic. We shrieked and gasped as we slithered in and thought we had to keep moving or we'd seize up and turn to ice. It must have done wonders for our stamina. Auntie Betty was very fit in those days and an excellent swimmer so we wanted to impress her but even so we didn't stay in long. She'd soon have us wrapped in towels to get warm – no tumble dryers in those days so the towels felt rough as doormats. After dressing, with teeth chattering and damp hair dangling, we shivered across the boards and met our father at the hot chocolate kiosk. He would always beat us to it and place an order for four piping hot chocolate drinks, served in funny plastic cups. I didn't really like the taste because it didn't taste like proper chocolate, but the smell was sublime.

The morning of the charity walk, starting with a short jog to get ahead of the mass of fund-raisers, that same sweet smell teased me – smooth, chocolatey and still sublime. When my legs started to tire and my feet ached it was thoughts of Auntie Betty which spurred me on. If charity walks had been the thing in her day *she* would have been at the front of the queue for a medal, and for a hot chocolate at the finish.

Hollie Hughes is a Children's Author, living and working in Essex. Her first picture book - *The Famishing Vanishing Mahoosive Mammoth* – will be published by Bloomsbury in 2016.

As well as picture book texts, Hollie also writes short stories and plays – and has had work shortlisted in a number of writing competitions.

Her audio drama – *A Leap of Faith* – was the overall winner of the 2014 Essex Book Festival 'Making Waves' competition. When not writing herself, Hollie enjoys running creative writing workshops for children – and has recently supported Kingston Primary School (Thundersley) to publish their first whole school anthology.

POTENTIAL

He had always known he was clever. Well, that is to say, he could not remember ever not being aware of being clever – which is not quite the same thing, but might as well be. He could though specifically recall the first time his mum had realised he was clever. He had just turned five, and the parents were invited in to look at their work in the classroom.

'Bloody 'ell, Jayden,' she'd said. 'You don't really get all this, do you?' She'd been looking at some maths work in his book.

He'd looked at her incredulously 'Of course I get it. What d'you think I am? A field mouse or something?'

It didn't quite register at first, but then she'd laughed. A kind of choking sound that had stuck in his mind for the next six years. It had taken him a while to work out why the laugh had sounded so strange, until finally he'd realised it was because it was the only time he'd ever genuinely heard her laugh at all. Of course, it wasn't the maths that made her choke – he knew that. It was the thing about the field mice.

It wasn't long after this that she'd signed him up to the football team. He accepted it as a kind of penance for being different, and because he'd felt sorry for her – even then. She would stand on the side lines, shouting until she went hoarse. The dads eyed her up approvingly - if only their own wives and girlfriends took such an interest. It was sad really, her being all on her own like that. Sometimes they tried to make conversation with her, and she'd smile and laugh. Never the real laugh though. Jayden was still waiting to hear that again.

Jayden's dad had not ever realised just how bright his son was. This was because, even if Jayden had bounced into this world calculating algebraic equations and reciting Shakespeare, Jayden's father would not even then have noticed. This was because Jayden's father had not stuck around past the first trimester – let alone until the due date.

By the time Jayden got to juniors, the football had stopped. He'd asked for books for his birthday. In fact, he'd helpfully supplied his mum with a list – children's literature not really being her thing.
'I haven't got the money for books, Jayden,' she'd said. 'All that football stuff ain't cheap you know – and you wouldn't like it if I bought you Tesco's own boots, would you?'

He'd quietly explained then that he didn't really like the football - never had done. Was unlikely, in fact, ever to do so in the future. He would much rather have the books, and he didn't care about brand names either – brand names were for losers who couldn't think for themselves. So she got him Nikes for his birthday – the cheapest ones you could get. But they said Nike on them, so that was ok. She didn't make him go back to football though.

The tuition centre was on the main road, just outside of town. Jayden knew where it was, because they'd passed it on the bus last summer holidays– when he'd had to go with her to the office cleaning job. She said it was best if he went to the classes on his own – the other kids might make fun of you, she'd said, if your mum takes you. He knew she was hiding something, but he didn't want to think about it too deeply. If a parent can keep a laugh from you, they could keep anything a secret, Jayden thought. And there were some things - some adult things - that Jayden at age 10 did not want to contemplate. Things that were just outside of his grasp, that he did not yet want to reach for. Not like the other boys in his class, tripping and falling over themselves to get close to adult secrets.

Of course, when he got there, he was the only kid not to be accompanied – just as he'd thought really. The tutor – Mr Merrill – seemed pleased enough to see him though.

'Ah, Jayden,' he'd said. 'Delighted, delighted . . . Yes, come in, come in, do sit down, we'll be starting in just a minute.' Jayden really hoped he didn't repeat everything he said like that. They started twenty minutes later, just as soon as the parents had all finished telling Mr Merrill how clever their kids were already.

When he got back that night, he'd asked her again. 'I told you Jayden,' she'd said. 'Why d'you have to keep on about it? I just happened to leave your report on the side at Ken's (from when I was getting my fags out – you know that) and, when I went back the next time, he said you had potential.' Potential. She sounded the word out slowly, as if she was teaching him something.

'Count yourself lucky – how much must Tom Shore's mum be paying out for his tutor?'

'Tom doesn't go to Mr Merrill – he goes to a proper tutor, in her house.'

She let it go. 'Ken said it's a shame, that's all – it's a shame to see all that potential going to waste.'

'Are you doing his cleaning for free now then?'

'He's not charging, Jayden. He's doing it to help.'

The trainers were wearing thin now, and he had to scrunch his feet up when he walked. He kept his toenails short, and his skin thick.

One night, after tuition, Mr Merrill told him to stay behind. He couldn't, Jayden said – he had to get back before mum went out again to her night shift. They only had one key, you see. Mr Merrill had bent down over the desk; close enough for Jayden to see the pools of yellow spittle forming in the corners of his mouth.

'You're not making it very easy for me to stick to my side of the bargain, Jayden' he'd hissed, straight into Jayden's face. His breath smelt sour, of coffee and fags – and frustrated opportunity. Jayden felt pretty sure he wouldn't have ever spoken to one of the paying kids like that.

Jayden sensed that the secrets were unravelling now, and that it would no longer be possible to put things back to how they were before – like a map that, once unfolded, would never lie factory flat again.

'No one gets anything for nothing, Jayden,' she'd snapped back at him that night.

'But you said we would get it for nothing though, didn't you? You said he wanted to help.'

She didn't answer then, just kept right on surfing her phone. The conversation was over, and he wouldn't ask again.

The next day, there was a fresh pair of Nikes waiting for him on his bed. Not the cheapest ones this time either.

Sometimes Jayden thought about the field mice. He thought that even the field mice must have realised where they were in the food chain – it didn't take a badger to work it out. He wondered at the lack of imagination on the teacher's behalf; that they might just as well have labelled them all 1-5.

The queue for the 11-plus wound all the way down to the corner, and into the next road. In spite of them saying he wouldn't see anyone he knew, Jayden found himself just a few families back from Tom Shore. They gave one another a self-conscious salute. Tom looked nervous. He didn't have to be - he hadn't been a field mouse. But then he hadn't been a badger like Jayden either.

They'd told him how it was all going to work a week before the exam. Not at the tuition centre – at Ken's house. He'd sat on the sofa dinking lukewarm orange squash, like a five year old. It was all a bit of a mix up, Mr Merrill had said. The other boy had been registered, but Jayden hadn't – something to do with the online registration.

'You know what I'm like on computers, Jay,' his mum had said.

Spent enough time on her new phone though, didn't she.

'Still – every cloud and all that,' Mr Merrill had said. 'No reason not to turn the situation to a mutually beneficial advantage.'

No one would even know who he was, they'd said. Just sign in, and use the other boy's details on the paper. Easy. Jayden's mum didn't even look up during this conversation - too busy surfing Sleepless Singles.

Tom was placed just across from him in the examination room. He looks like he's going to puke, Jayden thought. Of course, Jayden was well aware of Tom's weak points – he'd been advising Tom's mum on the 11-plus forum all through the summer. Well, 'absentlewis' had. Tom had needed lots of help with his verbal and non-verbal reasoning and, even now, his mum was worried he might not make it. The 11-plus forum site was an invaluable source of information and support – and not just for the 11-plus practise papers either. Everything you needed to know about online registration, right down to the programme for the day itself, were all there for the taking. Jayden could feel the scrunched up printout of the other boy's name and number in his pocket, pressing into the top of his thigh. A reminder. Jayden was thankful it wasn't Tom Shore's name on that bit of paper. He didn't think he'd have been able to go through with it if it had been.

'Turn your papers over now, please.' Jayden took one last glance over at Tom, gave him what he hoped was a reassuring smile, picked up the brand new HB pencil that Ken Merrill had sent him with, and began to write.

Name: Jayden Lewis Turner. Registration Number: 3781

He didn't think his mum would mind - not really. Not in the end. And what could they do about it anyway? In fact, Jayden was even daring to hope that he might yet hear that choking little laugh of hers again before this year was out. After all, what did they think he was? A field mouse or something?

Born in Essex in 1978, **Rob Shepherd's** published work includes the poems; "I am only Me" printed in *Forever Spoken* and "Heaven" featured in *The Best Poems & Poets Of 2007* published by ELY in association with Poetry.com.

Rob was awarded a fellowship into, and Recognised as a Poet Fellow Of Noble House Publishers.

To date Rob has written 6 books which include the poetry trilogy *The Human Condition! vols. 1-3*, The humorous fictional book *Life With Boris Karloff!*, short story e-book *Field Of Hope* and The Human Condition vols. 1-3 anthology book *A Human Condition.*

Rob has made several small online videos and short films, all available on YouTube.

Rob is currently working on several more titles of varying genre.

River Of Tears

Thomas walked up the road with Benji. Benji was a lot of work, being a rescue dog, he required a lot of attention and patience. Two things Thomas didn't really feel like extolling today. He would rather be home, in the warm, playing Skyrim on his computer. But thanks to his late arrival from school, due to a detention he'd earned from a fight with the eternally stupid and annoying Damian, he wasn't playing Skyrim. None of which he'd started let alone deserved to be on the end of the punishment for, but he had finished it, that was something at least. But this was his parents extended punishment for getting detention. That was the mad part of it. They hadn't been angry at him for getting into a fight, they had been more angry that he had detention. That he couldn't work out.

So here he was walking up the bridge that took them past the Council Offices. As determined as Thomas was to get home as quick as possible, Benji was equally determined to sniff and urinate against every parking meter along the pavement. And along this bridge there were more than enough to ensure that this part of the walk was going to take a damn while longer than Thomas had any patience for. "Oh come on Benji." Thomas growled as loudly as he could without drawing any more attention to himself than he had already attained.

Slowly, they made their way along the bridge, past the junction for New Road and down towards Argent Street. Thomas hated this part of Grays. The high rise buildings always made him feel uncomfortable and worried. There were always guys waiting around the edge of the greens around them, smoking joints with much bigger and fierce looking dogs than Benji. But Benji loved walking this way, mainly so that they could walk along the sea wall. Well, they called it the sea wall, but it was in fact the gateway end of the river which wound its way up towards Purfleet and up to Gravesend and Dartford. On clear days, they could see perfectly across the river to both. The only part of these walks that Thomas enjoyed. Seeing the container ships slowly trundling their way to dock and wondering what cargo they were carrying, even imagining some new, incredible cargo, after all, you never know right?

The pair had just past the junction and were just passing Seabrook Rise to their left, when Benji stopped all of a sudden, almost causing Thomas to get pulled clean off his feet and land backside first, had he not put his foot out and turned to steady himself. By the time Thomas had secured his footing and looked down, Benji was already squatting down on the small verge of grass, with his head pointing up to the sky, squinting, as though looking up to the cloudless sky for something. "Oh no, Benji, not here, really? There's a whole damn field just over there." Thomas sighed and pulled a poop sack out of the small holder clipped to his belt. He didn't much enjoy walking Benji at the best of times, but he hated having to clear up after him. It was horrible, stinky and now he was going to have to carry the stink with him until they got to a dog bin, which wasn't until they had crossed over Argent Street and almost to the sea wall itself. Gradually, with the smell barely being held inside the bag, the pair finally made their way up the small path from the field and up onto the walkway alongside the river.

Thomas binned the bag and bent down, taking the leash of Benji and letting him walk around, excitedly following wherever his nose lead him towards a possible spot of interest. Thomas trudged slowly behind him. One eye on what Benji was doing, the other on what the river and whatever was in or on it, was doing. The tide was out and he could see the dirty mud that lead up to the break slabs up against the wall itself. The mud could really smell bad, even worse that Benji's turds, and he Thomas had decided that Benji's poo was just about the smelliest thing on the face of the planet. They walked past the marina and on towards the expensive river front apartments. He could just about make out the wreck poking through the mud to his left and to his right was a concrete jetty, which lead up to the floodgates. Themselves apparently the only thing protecting the town from disaster should the river overflow. Not that he had ever heard of a time when it had. It was always far too low. Even at high tide. But he had heard the flood alarm go off on more than one occasion beside the usual test sounding. But he had always been indoors at the time and well, they lived well away from danger, half way up a hill, so he had never had any cause to worry. And besides which, his mum and dad had always told him about not worrying, saying how there had been special measures in place to stop anything ever happening.

It wasn't impossible, they had told him, but the odds were so high as to be ridiculous. Benji suddenly bolted forward, running up to the Jetty and barking loudly, growling in between barks. It snapped Thomas out of his daydream, causing him to rush to Benji's side.

"Benji. Stop it, you'll get us told off."

But Benji was still worked up and continued his startling aggression toward something that Thomas couldn't see. Not yet anyway. He crouched down to him, "What is it boy, what have you found? Better not be another crab or something, cause I swear, if it is, me and you have got serious talking to do."

It was just at that moment that something moved in corner of Thomas' eye, causing a splash of the remaining pools of water, standing on the surface and a distinct slap and squelch, which Thomas knew had to be the sound of the river mud being pushed aside and something squishing through and down into.

Thomas turned to cast his gaze in the direction of the sound and caught the sight of something grey, despite the mucky river mud that would clearly be clinging to it from crawling and slithering through it, he noticed, just briefly that it was most definitely a grey skinned creature. As to what it was, Thomas couldn't make out, it moved too fast, by the time he had seen it and acknowledged that he was seeing something real, it was gone again, leaving Thomas to ponder it for a few moments.

Meanwhile, Benji continued to growl and bark at something below him on his side of the jetty. Thomas sidled up to Benji to try and reassure him and calm him down, but it also meant that he might get another look at this thing, if it was the same thing that they were both seeing, or saw. Before Thomas could look down to find out, Benji lept up and backwards, yelping a panicked shrill before taking off, back from where they had come.

Thomas looked back in his own panic but before he could even utter a sound Benji had long gone. Worried for both Benji's safety (and his own should he return home to his parents without Benji, an injured Benji or worse), Thomas jumped to his feet in order to rush after him, but just as he did, his jeans felt like they had caught on something. Typical, he'd snag his jeans just when he needed to run after the dog and save him from danger. Spinning his head round and down to see where his jeans were caught up so that he could free himself he saw what it was and it wasn't a piece of scaffolding pole from the safety barrier to prevent him from falling in to the dirty river muck. He let out an ear piercing scream. And desperately tried to pull away. But it was no good, the grey, sloppy, smelly and muddied hand of some horrible, fearsome, gruesome creature, reached through the bars, gripping tight to his trouser leg, unwilling to let go of its seeming prey. Of all the times and places to die, he definitely didn't want it to be known at the tender age of 13 and down in the disgusting depths of the mud from the river.

Thomas pulled his leg with all of his strength, but just as he thought he had gotten free, the hand had merely readjusted its grip, this time managing to grasp the part of his leg just above the ankle that it had must have intended in the first place and now not only was it stronger and tighter than ever before, but before Thomas could realize that it was too late to do anything about his unfortunate situation, the hand pulled his leg hard, hard enough that what grip he had with the other foot was broken and he slid along backwards before toppling forwards with the sudden change of momentum being exerted upon him and he slid across the ground backwards. Thomas scrabbled desperately with his hands, trying to grasp anything he could to hold on to and save himself with, his fingers scraped along the gravel path and across the concrete, safety moving further and further from his reach. Down he slid, backwards through the lowest gap in the railings towards the mucky, sticky, gooey and stinking viscous muck of the river mud.

With one last gasp ditch attempt at escape, Thomas twisted himself, trying to flip himself over and find a way to pull himself free, but his timing was off and he lifted his head just as it was about to pass below the bottom railing. Without warning and without a clue as to the pending danger, the sliding of his body caused his head to slam forehead first, up against it, the resulting thud caused both a ring to vibrate through the barrier and a ringing in his ears. But that was to be short lived and replaced with a swirling motion in his head before everything suddenly turning pitch black, as though someone had flicked off the light switch to his mind.

It was sometime before Thomas awoke again but when he did, it was sudden, as though he hadn't even gone out. Where was he? He wondered. Was he still alive? Or was this death? Was this what it was like to be dead, especially for those who drowned? The dark surrounded him, but yet he could hear what sounded like water, wind, tides, life going about its business. If this was death, it was cruel and unusual punishment for a young boy who hadn't done anything bad, not really, only small things like any teenager. Even though he couldn't see a thing, instinct drove him to keep swinging his head around, looking, for something, for anything, a small something, just to see it. A sudden burst of light from a corner startled him. But nothing like what came behind it. Something incredible, something gross, something terrifyingly different to anything and anyone else.

Closer it moved, ever closer and Thomas felt around, attempting to find a way to at least distance himself from it. But there seemed to be no way to avoid this awful meeting, there seemed to be no way back from this encounter, this unspoken agreement that he'd not agreed yet had still seemed to have silently entered into. The thing slithered, slid and drew in close to Thomas, peering at him, casting it's beady eyes across him, head to toe. It's skin was smooth as silk, a perfect marine, shadowy Grey. The same perfect combination of the river mud, black-grey, viscous and terrifying, hiding an unknowable amount of secrets from an equally mysterious and unknown lifespan. *If* it was or had ever been alive.

"Who? *What*.are you?"

The creature, humanoid but unlike any person he had ever seen, even on those "world's weirdest" videos online, didn't answer, instead it simply exhaled, breathing out with a mixture of humanity and reptilian curiousness. Yet he could not mistake the underlying sensation, the message, of very real danger behind it. Then one by one pairs of eyes began appearing from every nook, every cranny, every recess and pocket inside what was now beginning to show itself as an underground, underwater/under-river chamber.

A figure from deep inside the space, (which Thomas could only now start to discern, split into numerous tunnels in every direction he could see, most probably leading to more chambers like this one), shuffled and seemed to jotter closer to Thomas. Again, its skin was much the same as the other was, grey, shiny, viscous, replicating the terrible mud at the bottom of the river. In it came, its face was something akin to human, but the rest of it was unlike anything Thomas could have imagined in his most vibrant and awful nightmares. It was the closest Thomas could think to absolute hell.

Each figure started to draw in closer to Thomas, their curiosity tied in all too obviously with their desire for ill. The first creature drew in close half growled, half hissed;

"We are the unknown. The different, the strange. We are the ones that your mum and dad never tell you about. We are here because we are the unwanted, the diseased, the sick, twisted, the mutated, the undesirable of this world. We are the unloved, the ignored, the feared and the loathed. Look at us. *Look at us*."

It continued, it's demands fulfilled by Thomas with hesitation.

"This is what you do. We are what your perfect life insists must happen. We are what your world creates in its insatiable appetite for new, for more, for perfect. We are the culmination of the disregard of you and your perfect poison up there have for itself. We are the unwanted, the un-loved. We are the abandoned. You see this? All this around you? This is here because we are. It is formed from the same process, the same ignorance and intolerance that creates us. And this?"

It/He, Thomas wasn't really certain which was correct, held out their hand, or what passed for one, and the grey-black viscous ooze that made up the river sludge seeped through its digits and dripped to its feet in long saliva like stringy strands of goo.

"*This*, this is the life, the birth, the womb that sustains us. *This* is our amniotic fluid if you will, our beginnings. And what creates it? All those that have been forgotten, abandoned, unloved, disregarded, left to die or killed by an unjust, un-caring inadequate world, *your world*. All the dead, they come here. The dumped, carcasses of those you toss away like used toilet paper. They come here, their *pain* comes here, it makes all this, it makes this and it makes us. And now *you* have come to us. *You* are to join us."

"I.I..I...I can't." Thomas stuttered, utterly terrified, both of it, of them and of what was to come, of what they meant.

"Come, come now Thomas. Do you think we don't know? Do you imagine that we are unaware of what happens, of what goes on up there? Do you think we don't have any clue as to what is going on right now? Of where you have come from? Do you really think that you ended up here by mistake? Think about it child. Think hard. Do your mum and dad *really* care? Does anyone really care about you up there? Has anyone, whatsoever, ever shown you the slightest bit of genuine attention and affection? Anyone at all? NO. Why? Because no-one gives a damn about you Thomas. Tom my boy. They couldn't care less, otherwise they would have someone looking for you. The police, coastguard, riverboats, divers, you name it. But where are they?"

"They, they don't know I'm down here, that's all. They, they haven't realised yet, but they will when I don't come home. Then they'll find me, you'll see."

Thomas tried to sound vaguely confident and just the tiniest bit threatening too.

"Really? Really Tommy? Are you sure? Because you've already been here for 3 days and not one person has even sniffed around here. Not even a crab has made enquiries for your tasty, malleable, adaptable flesh. You're one of us already Tommy boy. You're abandoned and you don't even know it, you don't even see that nobody gives a damn about you."

Tommy resisted it as much as he could. He tried to resist the urge to agree and to cry. But his heart sank and it hurt. It hurt like a train was sitting on it and crushing it to a pulp. The pain was excruciating. And it was so, because it was true. Nobody gave a damn up there, especially not about him. After all this time, all these years, it was all true, they all ignored him, save to shout, scream deny him and to push him out of the way. To bully him into silence and invisibility. Well now he *was* invisible and they still didn't care. His eyes welled up to meet the level of pain inside of him and the unleashed a torrent of pent up frustration, pain, hurt and loneliness.

That's it boy, you let it out. Those tears, feed the life, feed the mother. Feed the river. Our life. This river of ours, our river of tears.

Nobody knew what happened to Thomas Moreland and nobody had been able to work out what had happened, when, how or why. They just knew that he had taken his dog Benji for a walk and never returned home with him. Benji the only returnee, pining at the door. To be met by a panicked and worried Scarlet Moreland. But after 3 years, their hope of finding their youngest son has disappeared along with him and they had moved away, moved somewhere else, moved on. Without him.

Thomas Moreland's body had yet to be discovered, but a wading, treasure seeking enthusiast, had pulled out a bunch of clothes from the mud that looked similar to those that had been described by the police, along with a dog lead. But nothing else. Save for realising that the river mud, when the water is out, seems to be a mecca for all kinds of strange animals. His eye caught movement from one of the odd old gaps in the sea wall that Thurrock Council, the Port Authorities among others had abandoned trying to seal long ago, because they always seemed to open up again almost immediately. He knew how odd this place was, how eerie it felt, how it played tricks on your mind and knew that this was the first sign of what he and his fellow crabbers called river madness or

"The muds" as they preferred to call them. And abandoned his own search for life and riches and climbed out, making sure he kept well clear of the edge of the wall. He didn't trust this place today and as strange as it sounds, it felt like this place didn't trust him either.

He made his way back home along the path, passing a young man coming the opposite way. He wanted to say something, to tell him to turn back, but somehow the words didn't get spoken and the two men simply exchanged glances, nods of acknowledgment and carried on their opposite ways.

The bench there looked inviting. The man, in his mid-thirties but weary, worn down and out by the ravages of life on the road, on the street, anywhere, where he might be acknowledged, spoken to, of cared about. Enough for just one day. Just one day. That's all he wanted. But it never came. It never would. He knew that. He pulled off the rucksack from his back, placed it on the bench, sat beside it, and pulled out the sleeping bag from the top. It was worn, smelly and yet good enough to keep his aching bones warm in the cold nights. Especially now he found himself on the riverside. The concrete jetty stared at him, like a big rock diving board. The river called to him like a ghost from his past. Then the young boy, handsome, but lonely looking came out from nowhere. His skin Grey and lifeless, but flawless and perfect.

"Are you lonely?" The boy called out.

He nodded.

"Me too, I lost my mum and dad. They left and now I don't know where they are. They left me. Would you like to be my friend?"

This had quickly gotten weird. But right now, his heart was broken, his soul felt destroyed and he knew that the world and it's "life" didn't care for him. Not anymore. He reached out his hand to the young boys own outstretched limb. And for the first time he felt like someone cared, even if it was just a little boy.

"Sssss" he began stuttering, "Ssso, wwwhat is y, y, your nnnn, name?"

"Thomas. But you can call me Tommy, we all do.

"We" He responded nervous. "Oh yes, we, we are all the same aren't we? Like me, we. We are all abandoned on the river."

"The bodies of the abandoned, and the killed found their way down here, where people passed every day, never knowing, never caring. People just didn't care. That's why they were there in the first

*place. The dead, the mutated, the diseased, the homeless. All abandoned. They were **the** abandoned. They ended up here, one way or another and stayed, out of peoples' sight, out of people's minds, out of the way. Even if you weren't dead or mutated, this place, this spot, it changed you. Made you something else. Something strange, something horrible, something terrifying, something evil. Their blood fed into the river. Their bodies broke down and built up again within the spot, within the mud. Their bodies fed the river, they were part of it, their minds, their bodies, their flesh, was the river. The river of blood, the river of Tears".*

Award winning author **Sue Moorcroft** writes contemporary women's fiction with occasionally unexpected themes. ***The Wedding Proposal,*** **Dream a Little Dream** and **Is this Love?** were all nominated for Readers' Best Romantic Read Awards**. Love & Freedom** won the Best Romantic Read Award 2011 and **Dream a Little Dream** was nominated for a RoNA in 2013. Sue's a Katie Fforde Bursary Award winner, a past vice chair of the RNA and editor of its two anthologies.

Sue also writes short stories, serials, articles, writing 'how to' and is a creative writing tutor at home and abroad.

Sue's latest book: The Wedding Proposa*l,* a story of what happens when Elle and Lucas, who split up four years ago, find themselves sharing a small boat in Malta for the summer. Lucas hates secrets and Elle has rather a lot, so it's a combustible situation.

Website: www.suemoorcroft.com.

Facebook: sue.moorcroft.3

Facebook author page
facebook.com/SueMoorcroftAuthor

Twitter @suemoorcroft

Google+: google.com/+Suemoorcroftauthor

LinkedIn:
https://www.linkedin.com/in/suemoorcroft

Naughty Forty

This is our home, where me, Richard and our teenage son Aiden live. A modest, ordinary house, red bricks, black slates, gardens back and front. There are even yellow roses around the door, cottage-style. Or Richard-style, perhaps I should say.

Roses round the door there may be – but, inside, a lounge like a bomb-site with no carpet, no curtains, and furniture permanently strewn with wallpaper samples. Pot plants cower like a sad little forest in the corner of the room and the lampshades have taken up permanent residence on top of the bookcase. The books are in a pile in the hall.

Aiden occasionally looks in with the kind of horror sixteen-year-olds reserve for other people's mess, says, 'I hope this is sorted for when my friends come round on Friday,' then disappears upstairs to the relative safety of his own room.

Richard, who likes a quiet and ordered life, is equally discomfited by the muddle.

'We've really got to get tidied up,' he frets, stacking wallpaper books to make space so he can sit down on the settee. 'I don't know why you had to take the curtains down and the carpet up right now – we're not even ready to strip the old paper off.'

'I'm waiting for you to make a decision about the new paper,' I point out mutinously, dragging the top book back off the pile. 'We're not making any headway at all.'

Richard collapses onto the settee, with a sigh. 'That's because you haven't suggested anything I like, and you hate all my suggestions.'

I leaf through the samples. 'Okay, so how about Peony Prairie? It's quite 'busy', but if we chose plain curtains to pick up the peony colour, and pale-blue paintwork as a contrast …'

'Peony <u>Prairie</u>?' he snorts. 'Since when did peonies grow on a prairie?'

'Erm …' I'm a bit stumped there, because it's Richard who knows about flowers. 'Does that matter?'

He takes the book to examine my vibrant, daring choice, then slaps his hands to his head. 'Too bright and lurid, we'll all develop migraines!'

'You have no style,' I snap, dragging out a different book. 'I mean, just look at your selection! What's this one? Cold Porridge? And Dried Mushroom? All from the Boringly Beige Collection, available at every DIY store?'

Richard's blue eyes brighten with aggravation. 'If you mean Oatmeal and Morning Mushroom, I think they're very tasteful. The clangy, clashing colours you're suggesting will get on our nerves in a fortnight, but my colour-scheme is classic, dateless, it'll last and last ...'

'That's what I'm afraid of,' I mutter.

There's one of those silences as we each hunch a cold shoulder and study our favoured combinations industriously. Then Richard slides a conciliatory arm around my shoulder. His voice is soft. 'What's the matter, Judy? What's got into you, lately? There's nothing wrong with the décor in here, really, is there? Taking the room apart and announcing that you want to transform it is just part of your sudden desire for complete change – your hair, your clothes, your hobbies. Is it because you've turned forty? There's nothing wrong with forty, you know. I reached it before you did!'

I flip through the wallpaper samples, tossing back my hair which is freshly highlighted with Ginger Light. 'There's nothing wrong with a bit of change, either. You ought to try it sometime.'

He withdraws his arm. 'You've been watching too many television make-over programmes.'

I wrinkle my nose. 'And all you watch are Soaps and the weather.'

His eyelids droop, wearily. 'It's a pleasant relief. All this aggro about decorating exhausts me.'

'Then you need a bit more exercise,' I advise smugly, and bounce youthfully upstairs to get ready for my Salsa dance class, teaming my turquoise trainers and pink tights because bright colours make me feel energetic.

Anyway, it's not that I'm so mad for change, it's that Richard's totally against it! Honestly, since he turned forty – yes, before I did! – he seems to have developed this craving for security and keeping everything the same. 'Nothing wrong with the décor, indeed,' I huff, pulling at my silver laces. 'It's been as it is for at least three years!'

With a quick pit-stop at the kitchen to glug down a fruit juice, I call, ''Bye,' and breeze out of the house to meet my friends at the dance class. There are generally quite a few men there, but you wouldn't catch Richard coming with me.

In fact, when I suggested it, he just said, 'Don't you fancy something slower?'

'No. I do not.' I huffed. I really like the Salsa with its hip-swinging rhythm, jiggle-jiggle. Not that I'm very good at it, but it's quite nice to 'do my own thing'.

Richard doesn't even seem to understand about me colouring my hair. What he doesn't seem to realise is that my hair is actually changing colour all on its own – and grey streaks aren't 'me', yet. And my dance class is good for me. And so is expensive face cream. And so will my new in-line skates be, when I've mastered more than *Eek! Crash!* moves on them.

If he doesn't want to join me in my new, active life, he can stay on the sofa and nap.

Crikey, forget the dancing and the fruit juice, it's been a frantic week at work, all lost orders, awkward customers and staff off sick, and I'm afraid I'm beat. Absolutely shattered. I did skate to work this morning to bump up my stamina, but ended up with bruised knees and grazed hands. So I didn't have much choice but to give Salsa class a miss this time.

Anyway, Richard's asked to see my latest suggestions for the lounge, and I need all my energy to summon up persuasive charm.

But, to be completely honest, I'm getting a bit tired of the lounge project. It seems to have taken over our lives with fabric swatches and paint cards.

So I begin without my usual vigour. 'How about Tangerine Dream for the walls, cream slubbed-silk swags-and-tails for the window, and Lemon Sherbet paintwork?'

Richard is big and warm beside me on the settee, and as we gaze at my latest example of chic, I find myself snuggling up and resting my head on his shoulder. 'What do you think?'

'Horrible,' he whispers. But he slides his arm around me and snuggles back.

I throw down my armful of samples resignedly and begin to pluck outlandish suggestions from the air. 'Or how about white, everywhere? White curtains, carpet, walls, then you wouldn't be able to complain it was too colourful.'

Richard grins. 'I'd prefer black all over, then you could dye your hair to match.'

I prod him playfully. 'Or a beige ceiling, beige walls and a beige carpet, nothing there we'd get tired of.'

'Or scarlet.' Richard tickles me. 'Scarlet and orange. And yellow. And blue. And purple. An entire rainbow painted on each wall ...'

Aiden's voice suddenly rings out, full of anguish, from the doorway. 'Oh *great!*'

Our heads swing round, and we regard our son in sheepish surprise.

Aiden strides into the room and begins feverishly shoving wallpaper books into the empty bookcase. 'Didn't you remember?' he cries in the kind of passionate wail which only a sixteen-year-old who keeps well out of the way of work and then is mortified when it isn't done, can emit. 'You said I could invite friends round tonight, for pizza and a video!' He pauses dramatically. 'I've invited *Erica*.'

Richard and I exchange duly impressed looks. Aiden's been sighing over Erica for the past four weeks.

Aiden tuts. 'And all you're doing is arguing about the redecorating, but not getting on and doing it.'

'So what's the problem?' I ask, struggling out from Richard's embrace to give Aiden my attention, deciding not to point out that a playful prod or a tickle or two hardly constitutes an argument. 'Bring your friends round. There are pizzas in the freezer.'

Aiden gestures around the room despairingly. 'How can I? Just look at this! How can I invite people round? Mum's clashing schemes battle Dad's stodgy ones every day, but no-one's resolved a thing.' He isn't usually fussy about the state of the house. Of course, *Erica* hasn't visited before. He ends, 'Honestly, since you've turned forty, you two, you've been unbearable, Mum trying to change everything and Dad resisting. You've been like naughty kids!'

He turns to fling himself from the room and I leap up, hands on hips to cry, *'Just you come back here and apologise, young man.'*

But Richard cuts calmly across me. 'Go get your friends, Aiden, give us an hour and we'll tidy up. Promise.'

Aiden halts, shuffling his feet and stuffing his hands in his pockets. His ears have gone red, a sure sign that he's properly upset. 'Oh. Well. Thanks. Sorry.'

'Come on.' Richard hauls me to my feet and gives me a quick hug. 'The boy's got a point; the whole thing's gone on too long. Let's carry the settee into the hall while we roll the carpet back down.'

It's a pretty frantic hour, but by the time Aiden shuffles back in looking sheepish, the carpet's down, the lampshades and curtains are up, and we're just carrying the settee back in. With him are three friends, and one, a pretty girl with her hair a mass of plaits, clutches shyly at his hand.

In order not to stare at this very interesting new development in my son's life, I survey the room, musing, 'Hmm, peaches-and-cream …'

Before I can finish the sentence, Richard is thrusting my jacket at me and grabbing his car keys. 'Right, Aiden, your mother and I are going now.'

'Where?' ask Aiden and I together, looking, I expect, equally amazed.

'Out,' he says, unhelpfully, hustling me through the door past Aiden's friends who are standing about waiting, no doubt, for the promised video entertainment to begin.

Aiden disengages himself from Erica to follow us. 'You must have some idea of where you're going?'

'Not yet,' Richard tosses over his shoulder.

'Well … what time will you be home?'

Richard unlocks the car. 'Before bedtime. You don't have to fret about us, we're old enough to look after ourselves.'

Safely in the car, leaving Aiden hands-on-hips on the doorstep, Richard winks at me. 'It's years since I've been called "naughty". It made me feel quite young. Dancing first, then the pictures? You can teach me this Salsa-thingy.'

I smother a yawn. 'Or how about a nice meal? After all that scurrying about with curtains and furniture I'm too whacked out for dancing.' And, imagine if we go to the pictures, and I fall asleep! I might snore.

But a meal in a nice restaurant with my husband sounds lovely. Just my kind of thing. Then I won't be too tired tomorrow to take all those sample books back to the wallpaper shop, because, honestly, the lounge looks fine as it is.

We don't need to redecorate.

We need to get out and enjoy our lives, while we're young.

Claire Buckle has been writing for about ten years and in that time her short stories have been published in the small press journals, Scribble and Ficta Fabula, magazines such as the Woman's Weekly Fiction Special, the Ireland's Own Anthology and the My Weekly Annual. She has undertaken creative writing courses offered by the Open University, the University of East Anglia, and has attended several workshops.

Apart from three years at a Polytechnic in Coventry, way back in the late '70's, Claire has lived in Essex all her life and in her Hornchurch home for the past 26 years. Aside from writing, she likes to paint in watercolours, attends weekly yoga and Pilates classes and loves long walks with her husband and energetic Cockerpoo, Phoebe, their favourite haunts being Hainault Forest and Hornchurch Country Park.

The world of writing is hard to break into and she wouldn't have been published without the invaluable support and feedback from the Brentwood Writing Circle, the Hornchurch based, Fairkytes writing group as well as Jan, Lucy and Chris, her close writing buddies. They deserve a big 'thank you.'

THANKS FOR THE MEMORY

Harriet climbed the stairs, grumbling at each step about her arthritic knees.

"I should have asked Margaret and Brian to bring the boxes down," she said, addressing the cat, which sat regally on the landing watching her progress. As if I haven't got better things to do than sort out old boxes, she thought. Really, they could all have been dumped as far as she was concerned. There'd be no room for much anyway once she was ensconced in the residential home. It was all her daughter and son-in-law's idea, of course.

"It's a lovely place Mum," Margaret had said, handing a glossy brochure to Harriet. It depicted glamorous elderly people, some sitting in a beautifully decorated lounge, others walking in the colourful landscaped gardens of the home, deep in the picturesque Essex countryside. "You'll have plenty of company and there are loads of activities going on – look." Margaret showed her mother a list at the back, "*everything from flower arranging to bingo.*"

"Hmmph." Harriet begrudgingly flicked through the brochure. "When have you ever known me to play bingo and, as far as I'm concerned, cut flowers are just dead ones. And, another thing, what about Tigger?"

Margaret persisted. "I've already told you, Tigger will come and live with us. No more worrying about where he's wandered off to. Besides, you'll see him when you come to us on Sundays." She moved across the sofa and put her arm around Harriet's thin shoulders. "Even if you're not interested in joining in, moving there will be for the best Mum, the stairs are a chore for you now and the garden's become a real worry."

"Well it wouldn't be if the gardener had done his job properly," Harriet replied. "I reckon I could do a better job myself even with my poor old joints."

"Don't talk nonsense, Mum." Margaret's voice was edged with impatience and she rolled her eyes upwards. Harriet suspected her daughter thought her an old grouch, but she had every right to be disgruntled. Three gardeners in a year and still not one of them had been anywhere near the standard Harriet expected. Eric used to cut the lawn into regimented stripes using a push mower and in the borders his salvias would stand to attention in rows, like red-coated soldiers.

Now there were problems with the cleaning lady. She refused to come any more after Harriet suggested she'd simply been spraying the polish around the room to trick her into thinking it had been cleaned. Harriet's eyesight wasn't too good, admittedly, but she was certain the sideboard had been left dusty. The house, a neat semi on the outskirts of Brentwood, had become such a burden, but she'd banked on Margaret suggesting she live with them. Not that she could manage in their town house, but with the money from the sale of her home they could have moved to one with an annexe. She told Margaret she'd seen plenty for sale on *Escape to the Country.*

But, Harriet was told; it was out of the question. Margaret liked her independence and still worked full-time. Besides, she and Brian weren't getting any younger and had plans to downsize when they retired in a few years' time.

So, after visits to several different retirement homes, Harriet agreed a move to *Lilac Lodge* would make her life a lot easier. In fact, the room on offer impressed her. It was spacious and tastefully furnished in pastel pink and pale apricot. Opposite the bed a large bow window overlooked a well-cared for lawn and colourful herbaceous border. Still, Margaret needn't know quite how chuffed she felt.

She'd left all the arrangements for the house sale to her daughter, who breezed in and out with a variety of potential buyers, finally announcing the house had been sold to the Graysons, a young couple of whom Harriet had initially disapproved because of the woman's obvious preoccupation with tattoos. However, when the pony-tailed husband enthused about how he loved the original features (apparently avocado bathrooms were the epitome of retro style these days) and his wife explained she was going to reinstate Eric's vegetable patch, Harriet's opinion had softened.

"Come on then Tiggs, we'd better take a look at these blessed boxes." Harriet puffed as she reached the landing. She paused for a moment to catch her breath and then pushed open the door to the bedroom, only to be confronted by just one multi-coloured box that had been placed in the middle of the bed.

"I thought Margaret said there was a lot to sort out," Harriet mumbled. Oh well, maybe she'd misunderstood. She eased herself down onto the bed, removed the lid of the box and peered inside. There, wrapped in delicate tissue paper, was the Christening shawl. Harriet lifted it out and carefully opened the protective layer. She held the soft wool to her face and inhaled. She could almost conjure up that wonderful scent, exclusive to babes in arms. She had been delighted to receive it from her mother, who'd spent many hours crocheting the lacy thread into a web of intricate patterns. Money had been tight and she and Eric would never have been able to afford such a beautiful item for the baby girl they'd finally been blessed with.

Hopefully her granddaughter, Gemma, might be as thrilled with it one day. She put the shawl down beside her and peered inside the box.

"What *has* Margaret been up to?" Harriet said to herself as she took out a folder containing paintings, drawings and poems that her daughter had written during her childhood. Amongst the other treasures was Margaret's first pair of shoes, a pretty pink baby's bonnet trimmed with appliquéd flowers which, Harriet remembered, a kind old aunt had knitted. Beside them was a small soft teddy holding a plush red heart that Harriet had been given by Gemma one birthday. Mothers' Day and birthday cards were tied into a bundle with a wide satin ribbon and underneath those were anniversary cards from Eric.

Dear Eric. She could look back on their happy marriage without the tears which once stingingly sprang into her eyes at the mention of his name. Fifty wonderful years together and then came the cancer that had stolen him from her life. Still, his end had been peaceful and pain free, thanks to the gentle care of their local hospice.

A large card nestled at the bottom of the box. Slightly curled at the edges, it proclaimed *Good Luck In Your Retirement* across the front. As she lifted it up, a small, cream envelope fell onto her lap.

The inside of the card was covered with messages of good wishes from all the pupils in her form.

To the best teacher anyone could ever have, love Karen xxx

She squinted at the small writing.

We will miss you Miss!! Love Janice.

Thanks for making the English and drama lessons such fun. Linda

Harriet smiled as she read all the lovely sentiments captured in time and preserved on the page. Goodness, all her pupils from her fifth form. She shook her head. The years since had flashed by.

Laid flat at the bottom of the box was a theatre programme.

"What have we here Tiggs?" Harriet said as she lifted it out. Her face creased into a broad smile.

"Well I never. *Cinderella. The Queen's Theatre, Hornchurch. December 1953.*"

She ran her hand over the cover – a simple line drawing of Cinders in her ball gown dashing down the staircase. Her hand shook as she turned the pages. There was an advert for *Elizabeth the Reigning Fashion House* in Corbets Tey Road, Upminster. What an appropriate a name, for that coronation year. Two pictures of women in elegant outfits, their full skirts with nipped in waists graced the page. She chuckled. She wasn't sorry when corsets went out of fashion. So uncomfortable! Mind you, Margaret could do with a bit of help with her tummy these days. Her mind wandered. Perhaps she should suggest Margaret try those magic knickers she'd seen advertised in the Sunday supplement. Then again, her daughter could get rather prickly sometimes. She abandoned the idea with a shake of her head.

She turned the page to the Synopsis of Scenes and list of musical numbers. It had been quite a production. Waves of memories washed over her. She gazed into the distance. She'd been in her early twenties, a teacher full of enthusiasm, eager to take her class to the newly opened theatre.

It was a special treat for the girls. How smart they looked – all turned out in their school uniforms. The headmistress insisted there were to be no casual clothes, despite it being an outing during the holidays. Those girls, all so well disciplined, or perhaps she was putting the pupils on a pedestal, conveniently forgetting how challenging youngsters could be? She smiled. She seemed to recall Mary Mclean became over-excited, had giggled endlessly and scoffed too many sweets during the first half. She'd been sick in the toilets during the interval. Still, Harriet managed to mop her up and sit her in the seat next to her own for the rest of the show. They were enthralled by the production and the thrill of seeing a live performance. How she loved the theatre. A pleasure she'd never grown weary of.

She'd already been with Eric to the Queen's Theatre. They were courting when they saw the first production, See How They Run, a month or two before the panto season started. She couldn't remember details but was sure it was a farce, something to do with vicars and mistaken identity. No programme in the box for that play, but no matter. She would never forget how Eric presented her with a corsage and how she'd lovingly pressed it within the pages of her parents' heavy Encyclopaedia.

She bent to fuss Tigger who was wrapping himself around her legs, when she noticed the envelope resting in her lap. The glue on the flap had gone hard and brown but the paper inside was still a perfect cream, folded neatly to fit the envelope. Harriet opened it up and read the looped script.

Dear Mrs Johnson,

This is just a little thank you note to say how much we appreciate everything you have done for our daughters over the years that you have taught at Romford County High. You brought such a fresh approach to your English lessons that we are quite envious we were never encouraged in the same way by our teachers! Susan, Angela and Barbara will always remember you with great affection. Susan, as you know, is now at Oxford University studying English Literature. No one in our entire family has ever been to university before, let alone to one of the best in the land. Had it not been for your inspired lessons taught with such enthusiasm she would never have achieved the results she needed for such a prestigious college. We all wish you happiness in your well-deserved retirement.

With kind regards,

Marian and Geoffrey Thomas

A lump caught in Harriet's throat as she carefully replaced the letter inside the envelope. She couldn't actually remember whether Susan was the one with the long auburn plait, or was that Denise who'd also gone on to Oxford, or was it Cambridge? Nowadays things could get a little fuzzy, faces merged and names floated away, just out of her reach, as though carried off on a breeze. Other times memories were so vivid and bright it was almost like watching those old Technicolor films she and Eric used to love snuggling up to at the pictures.

Harriet carefully placed everything back into the box. How sweet of Margaret to gather together such a cornucopia of treasures and release so many memories from the dusty silence of the loft. It must have taken quite some time to sort through so many old cardboard boxes and find the most poignant belongings. As she slowly got up from the bed Tigger began to meow.

"And you can stop your complaining. You're a very lucky boy to be going to live in a house with a lovely big garden, and no doubt getting spoilt rotten. Now, no more moaning thank-you!"

Harriet went downstairs carefully holding the banister as she descended, stopping at the bottom to steady herself before heading for the kitchen. She could do with a reviving cup of tea. As she waited for the kettle to boil, she took the brochure from the kitchen table and turned to the back. Picking up her pen, she looked down the row of activities. She may not have as much physical energy now as in the past but she could make up for it in enthusiasm and experience. Hoping her involvement over the years in school plays and all those sixth form reviews would be appreciated, she circled one halfway down. *Lilac Lodge Residents' Amateur Dramatics Club.* Time, Harriet thought with a grin, to get the show on the road.

ANNE CASSIDY lived in London for most of her life. She worked in a bank for five years but then became a teacher. In 1989 she started writing books for teenagers. She has published over forty novels for young adults. She writes dark crime fiction and is best known for her book ***Looking for JJ*** which was shortlisted for the Carnegie medal. ***Moth Girls*** was published by HOT KEY in Jan 2016 and concerns the disappearance of two twelve year old girls. Her new novel ***No Virgin*** is just out and describes the aftermath of a rape.

THE WORD OF LOVE

The sign on the front of the bookshop is The Word of Love. Alma thinks it's clever, a play on words. George thinks Alma is clever. And beautiful. And efficient.

George Bailey, on the other hand, is none of these things. He knows because Alma tells him frequently; not in so many words but in directed sighs and poisonous looks. One morning, at breakfast, among a small mountain of newspapers he misplaces his glasses. A few minutes later he finds them down the side of an armchair and using the end of his shirt, polishes each lens until it glitters. It's important, George thinks, to see the world clearly.

Alma is overseeing these events while fidgeting with her earrings and scratching a red area of skin on her neck. Haven't you got a clean shirt, she says. You've let yourself go, she says. You don't want to go into the shop looking like that. George looks down at his shirt. Except for a tea stain near his pocket it's perfectly clean looking. He combs his fingers through his hair and looks at Alma's pale blue eye shadow and carefully drawn pink lips and thinks she hasn't aged a day in twenty years.

Alma can't take her eyes off George's hands on the newspaper. His fingers are fat and look like chipolatas. She smiles, thinking of the long thin fingers of the publisher's rep, Terry. And his small bottom that she seems to be able cup with both hands. Alma hasn't touched George's bottom for many years. The thought of it brings on a mild nausea.

You just don't look after yourself, she says, You're old before your time.

Alma is further annoyed. George has lost the paperwork for the publisher's rep. George thinks it's inside one of the books on the shelves. He picks through dozens of hardback romances that he and Alma have collected over the years. Their covers are dusty and untouched but he still opens them, touching their yellowing pages with tenderness.

A photograph drops out of one of them and floats to the floor. He picks it up and his face takes on a look of astonishment. He looks across the book shop past the PLEASE PAY HERE sign at the figure of Alma.

Alma wraps a book for a customer and does not notice her husband's stare. Her bracelets jangle as she rips off strips of sticky tape and binds the paper bag as though it contained a wad of fifty pound notes and not just a paperback book.

In the drawer, underneath some books, she notices the forms for the publisher's rep. She takes them out and runs her fingers back and forth over the typewritten surface. She raises them up to her face and inhales deeply. She fancies his cologne is still there, lingering, sweet and heavy and she drinks it in.

She knows George is still looking for these papers but she leaves him to it. George is always happier when he has something to do, she knows that.

George sits down on a footstool behind the shelves of books. There is a large hardback open on his lap. George doesn't look at the cover, has no idea what the title is; just another Victorian romance.

In the middle of the book there is a photo of Alma that he has never seen before. Alma in one of her best dresses, her hair piled up on top of her head, her long painted nails holding a stemmed glass of something.

George is frowning because there is something quite strange about this Alma, in the photograph. He's seen the dress, he's seen the hair, he's watched the interminable painting of the nails. No, these are not odd at all.

Alma is *smiling*. It isn't a grin. It's a warm gleeful smile and it makes Alma look like somebody George has only just met and doesn't really know.

He turns the photo over. On the back, in Alma's writing, are the words, *I love you Terry.*

What's going on, George! He hears Alma's voice from the far end of the shop.

He should show her this photograph, insist on knowing where she was going, what it is all about, who this Terry is, what the smile was for. George feels a mounting panic in his chest.

George! He hears Alma's strident voice. He raises his shoulders in defence. Mr Bannister will be here soon, she says. You need to take over the till. George? Have you fallen asleep?

He hears her heels clicking along the wooden floor and he turns the photo over. *I love you Terry.*

Terry, Terry, Terry. He could almost hear Alma's voice gasping the name. He would ask her about it. No, he would demand to know.

And then she was there standing in front of him, her skirt creased across the middle where she had been sitting at the till, her tights wrinkled over her knees, the points on her shoes looking delicate and deadly at the same time.

What are you doing round here, George? She says with a voice like stone.

George looks up at her. He wants to grab her scraggy legs and hit her and hit her until she bruises.

George are you ill? She says, her words softer, crumbling like pebbles.

Then he wants to put his arms around her hips and hug her to him. He wants to push his face into her belly and smell her talcum powder. He wishes then that he had put on a clean shirt that morning.

George, pull yourself together. Mr Bannister will be here in a minute.

He stands up and turns away from her, replacing the photograph inside the book back on the shelf. The shop door bell rings and a male voice shouts, Alma? Are you there?

Alma hears the voice and smiles as though a champagne bottle had just been uncorked.

George turns to say something but Alma is striding out, straightening her skirt, pulling her sweater down over her hips, fluffing her hair out with her fingertips.

Mr Bannister, you're early! She says and her words are like little balloons that bounce along in the air. George, you look after the till will you? I'll be as quick as I can. I'm sure Mr Bannister is a busy man.

Mr Bannister looks edgy and keeps passing his brief case from one hand to the other. He is thin and barely fills his own suit. He avoids eye contact with George and follows Alma behind the counter into the shop storeroom. A click sounds and George knows that a key has been turned.

He sits at the till and runs his hand along the counter that she has touched. Breathing in deeply he is sure he can smell her perfume.

It's the most he can hope for, George knows that.

Liz Trenow - About the author

Liz Trenow is a best-selling author and former journalist who spent fifteen years working for regional and national newspapers, and for BBC radio and television news, before turning her hand to fiction. Her three novels, *The Last Telegram, The Forgotten Seamstress* and *The Poppy Factory,* are published by Harper Collins UK. She has also been published in America and a number of European languages.

Her work is highly acclaimed: *The Forgotten Seamstress* reached the top twenty of the New York Times best-seller list, *The Last Telegram* was nominated for a national award and sales of *The Poppy Factory* took it into The Bookseller's weekly 'heatseekers' list for nearly two months. She is a popular speaker at the Essex Book Festival and other festivals around the country.

Liz has just completed her fourth novel, *The Master Piece,* which, as with some of her previous novels, draws on her unique background for inspiration. Liz's family have been silk weavers for nearly 300 years and she grew up in a house next to the mill in Sudbury, Suffolk, which still operates today.

Liz lives in Colchester, Essex with her artist husband and has two grown up daughters. Find out more at www.liztrenow.com and join her on Twitter @LizTrenow.

Coming Back

Enid drifted in and out of consciousness, bound to the bed by a tangle of wires and bleeping machines, and dreaming vividly.

She dreamed of her own funeral: black-clad relatives solemn at the graveside, rain falling softly, the grass luminous green, dark gravestones glistening with lichen. Her brother Brian and her son Sam stood stiffly in ill-fitting suits, their faces tight with repressed emotion. Only Lisa, her granddaughter, was openly weeping.

From her aerial view she could even see the gravediggers having a cigarette, sheltering from the rain under the eve of the chapel. At the back of the graveyard, behind yew trees blackened by rain, was a stranger in a red raincoat. She had a powerful feeling that there was something she ought to know about this person, but was woken by the harsh ring of the ward telephone before she could decipher it. Now she would never find out.

Another time Enid dreamed of her own death. It was a strange experience, floating above the surgeon's table, looking down at her poor baggy body, the green-clad crowd around it.

'She's gone, leave it John.'

'No, give it a minute more.'

'Keep going.'

'She's done this before and come back.'

She did not want to come back, but something was pulling her and she couldn't resist it. And then there she was in her body again, the searing whine of the monitor modulating into a gentle, regular bleep. Her heart was pumping, consciousness returning. And the pain with it.

'Let me go,' she tried to shout. No sound came out, but the nurse noticed.

'All right Enid,' she tried to soothe. 'Relax now, we'll make you comfortable.'

The old man in the bed next door was snoring. 'Perhaps I'm supposed to be dead,' she thought. 'Why did I have to come back?' She opened her eyes and found Brian standing at the bedside with bunch of flowers, a big grin and the smell of fresh air floating around him.

'Welcome back sis. Thought we'd lost you this time. But you're a tough old bird, aren't you?'

Enid did not want to be called a tough old bird. She wanted to tell him how offensive this sounded, given her tender state of health, but the words would not come out. Just a short while ago, she thought, I was looking forward to eternity. Now here I am in an uncomfortable hospital bed full of wires and drips, with the man still snoring beside me and my brother calling me unflattering names. She scowled at him till he turned away and went to talk to the pretty nurse.

Later, Lisa arrived looking like something from the operatic underworld, with her black hair and pale face – her Goth look, she'd once explained – fearlessly pushing aside the wires and drips to give her grandmother a warm hug. Her touch alone made Enid almost glad to be back. She opened her eyes.

'Granny, you're awake. Thank goodness. You've been asleep the last few times I've come. Can you talk? No, never mind. Just wink at me and I'll know you are hearing me. How do you like my dress?'

She did a twirl in her full-length floaty black lace number, fresh off the rack in a local charity shop, Enid assumed. It reminded her of widow's weeds. Just as well I can't talk, she thought, or I'd probably tell her what I think, and offend her.

The man in the next door bed opened his eyes and started to moan loudly as Lisa came into his field of vision. He cried out in a panicky voice: 'No, not yet, not yet'. Perhaps he thought Lisa was the grim reaper. 'It's just my granddaughter,' Enid wanted to reassure him, but Lisa was there first. She calmed him down, and called the nurse. Then she returned to Enid, took her hand and stroked it. There were tears in her eyes.

'We do love you, Gran. Keep on fighting, won't you?'

Later still, or perhaps it was the next day, Enid woke to the sight of Lisa, Sam and Brian walking down the ward towards her bed, with a stranger in a red raincoat.

Lisa was first at her bedside: 'Gran, you won't believe it, this is Marianne, she's come all the way from Australia to find us. Her mum was adopted and she thinks you could be her granny. It's so weird, we might be cousins! Oh, sorry, formalities first. Marianne, this is Gran. She can't talk but she can hear everything we say, so just act normal.'

'Mrs Barclay?'

****

Five years of looking and I seem to have found my English family: an uncle, a great uncle, even a wacky cousin into the bargain. And now my gran.

I always knew Mum was born in England but it was only just before she died that she told me she'd been adopted. After the funeral, life just seemed so empty. I needed to know more about the woman I'd lost, the woman who made me who I am. It became my mission – in danger of becoming an obsession, my friend Annie suggested. If I could find out where she came from, who were her birth parents and why they gave her up, I would be able to accept her loss and get on with my life. I scoured the libraries in Sydney, spent hours on the net, ran up a huge bill on international calls. Then one day, when I was at a real dead end, and my money running out, I got an email from English social services.

There was an address, too, but no phone number. I wrote, but my letters came back: 'not known at this address'. International enquiries produced nineteen possible contacts in that area of Essex, and I phoned them all. Some failed to answer, some were rude and others friendly. But none of them knew an Enid Barclay.

I was even more determined than before. I worked double shifts and waited on tables to raise the cash. I even took out a bank loan, even though Annie told me I was crazy. Finally I managed to get enough together for the airfare. When I left Sydney it was 40 degrees in the shade. I was so glad to be on that plane for England.

When I arrived in the UK it was raining, a cold sleety November rain, and dark at four o'clock in the afternoon. I'd never been to London before so I caught a taxi. What a great taxi, so high off the ground, lovely smell of leather seats, and such a chatty driver. I really felt I was on the way to finding my family, at last.

The traffic was dreadful. We've got traffic but nothing like this. The journey took hours and the taxi cost a fortune. I was pretty depressed when I finally got here. All the time I was so afraid I'd have come all this way and not find my family, or they would all have died.

That night I stayed in a cheap hotel room and had a nightmare about a funeral. In my dream it was raining like hell with lots of people in black and these big gloomy trees everywhere. I was wearing my red raincoat – the one I bought in Sydney after Annie suggested I ought to wear something bright so people could see me in the English smog. For some reason I began to understand that it was my granny's funeral and started to panic, trying to shout: 'No, not now, you can't die now'. But I couldn't make a sound and no-one turned round. It was horrible, feeling imprisoned in this red coat and unable to move in case I was seen and told to leave.

I woke myself up shouting.

You wouldn't believe the rigmarole I went through at the Town Hall, looking through the electoral register to find the address of every Barclay. It took nearly half a day. And then I started slogging round the streets: all unwelcoming doorways and drawn curtains. At home no-one ever closes the curtains. Still it's not surprising when you think how cold and dark it is here.

At the first four places either no-one answered, or they gave me blank stares and shook their heads. At the fifth address – a tiny house in a row of identical houses attached on either side and all butted right up on the street – it took a very long time to open and, when it did, there was this frail little old man. When I said the name he smiled. 'Come in out of the rain my dear, you'll catch your death.'

Once I got inside and managed to explain who I was looking for, he smiled again, more sadly this time. 'You've got the right place, my dear. My name is Brian Barclay and Enid is my sister, but I'm afraid you may be too late. She's in the hospital, and gravely ill.'

****

As Enid tried to focus her gaze on the woman in the red raincoat the fog in her brain began to clear. There was something about the face that she recognised. It was the eyes, the clear, pale blue eyes of Edward, the soldier she once loved, who went to war and never returned. Enid had wiped him from her consciousness, but now the memories came flooding back.

'I have been trying to find you for years. I think I am your granddaughter,' the woman said.

The reality was dawning slowly, but it was too much to take in. Enid tried to smile, to nod her head, but she didn't seem to have any control over her muscles. Lisa was hopping up and down with impatience.

'Gran, this is sooo important! Can't you try to speak? Or perhaps if I hold your hand….perhaps you can press it? Is she right, did you really have a child who was adopted? Do you know her?'

Suddenly, Enid was overwhelmed with the need to live, to relive that lost moment of her life. She had been just seventeen, and had loved Edward so fiercely that when he died she felt she must die too. As soon as the baby arrived it was taken away, and she had never been able to grieve for the child or her lost lover. In time they had just become a small blank space buried deep inside her.

Yet here was her daughter's daughter, in flesh and blood, and Enid couldn't even find the voice to answer her. But she could press Lisa's hand with her thumb. The first time she did it, Lisa jumped as though she'd had an electric shock.

'Yes! She pressed my hand! Oh Gran, is she really your granddaughter? Tell us all about it…oh I wish you could.'

Tentatively, the woman came closer to the bed, and took Enid's warm, frail hand in hers. There were tears in her eyes. And, finally, Enid's own tears began to flow, slipping down the side of her face and onto the pillow.

This is what she had come back for.

Sue Dawes completed an MA in Creative Writing in 2010 and since then has had some success in writing competitions, with her stories published on-line and in magazines. This year she won Criminal Lines, for the first 15,000 words of a novel. Sue writes in many different genres including science fiction, literary fiction, crime fiction and a bit of magical realism, of which the Witch's Bottle is an example.

Primarily a mum, in her spare time, as well as writing, making jewellery and bookkeeping, Sue edits and produces a free writing pamphlet for commuters, called Words-Down-The-Line.

A member of three writing groups, she also contributes and administers a blog called : http://wivenhoewriters.blogspot.co.uk.

The Witch's Bottle

The spirit in the bottle
Go softly where ye tread
The lady is a cunning one
Disturb ye not the wicked dead

Never tarry on a restless night
Lest ye find what darkness means
For she will trouble thee until in sleep
And steal thy soul through dreams.[1]

Friday 13th

When I release the bottle from the clod of soil that wraps it, I know it is different. It's smooth, made of opaque, green glass aged by a thousand tiny, hair-line cracks. I fancy that if I count the fractures, it will take me back to the date it was buried. I hold it up to the failing light and run my calloused finger over its rough, cork-stopper.

I think I have seen something like the bottle before, in St Osyth's Priory Museum. I try to remember the monkish script that labelled the display but these days my memories are as hard to catch as dandelion clocks. The words come to me

---

[1] The Witches Warning

http://myths.e2bn.org/mythsandlegends/textonly20-a-witch-in-a-bottle.html

slowly *Witch's bottle. May contain human hair, bent pins and urine.* I think I remember it because it sounds like one of those new-fangled warnings they put on everything; *may contain nuts.*

I shake the bottle gently, expecting to hear its contents whisper back but it is empty. I examine the base which I hit several times with my garden spade, thinking it was just a chunk of stone preventing me from finishing my job here, at the Priory. The only evidence is a tiny scratch. It's as if the glass has pushed the damage back.

I place the bottle onto the ground, next to the plot I have half-dug. For a second I think I see something moving inside, a grey mist, but I realise it is just light bouncing a reflection from a break in the clouds. I rub the base of my spine before I continue digging. Tiredness and old age are making me whimsical.

It's dark when I eventually get home to my own garden. These days it seems to take twice as long to do anything. I hang up my gardening coat, pull off my damp Wellingtons and place the gardening tools neatly against the wall in the shed. I shut the shed door behind me. I forget about the bottle in my coat pocket.

Saturday 14th

The first time I hear the voice it is a wisp of sound carried in by the morning breeze. It drifts past me as I open my bedroom window to let the night out.

> *"Let me go."*

I don't remember who the voice belongs to. Perhaps I imagine the words from my neighbour's wrinkled mouth: she often believes she is imprisoned, or that her son is trying to poison her. Or maybe I assume it is breakfast television blaring its usual good morning through the walls of my terraced house. I might even think it is static playing around in my hearing aid.

The second time I hear the voice I am downstairs buttering my wholemeal toast. This time it is more of a buzzing, the words flitting gently around my eardrum.

> *"Let me go."*

The third time it interrupts me as I am scouring the dictionary for a four-letter word that will complete the morning crossword.

> *"Let me go."*

I put down my pencil. The words have got my attention, murmured in the draft that squeezes through the back door.

I ease myself out of the carver chair and walk stiffly across the linoleum. Where are they coming from?

Exchanging my slippers for slip-on shoes, I fiddle with the bolt on the back door, before flinging it open. Fresh air greets me, caressing my sun hardened skin like an old friend.

"Let me go. I do not belong here."

The voice is as clear as the sky, and as light as the swallows skimming it. I walk towards the sound, trying to find its source, past my vegetable plot; with its tangled tepee of beans and flowering peas. It becomes more insistent as I reach the shed. Have I left Radio 4 on?

"Let me out. Let me out"

It reminds me of a nursery rhyme.

The shed door is ajar. I must have forgotten to shut it last night. I open it wide and let the sunlight swell in. A ladybird lands on my shoulder, clambering sleepily onto my hand. I transfer it carefully to an earthenware pot. I look at the neat shelves of seeds and twine, Jeyes fluid and Maxi crop. The only life inside is a spider spinning its web.

"Let me out."

It is a dreadful, desperate sound and I shudder despite the warm April sun.

"They burned me. The men in black. Help me..."

I feel its anguish but I cannot see where it's coming from.

I walk towards my neighbour's fence, wonder if their overgrown garden is hiding an injured cat or one of those awful electronic toys set to play until the batteries run out. Maybe it's the fence posts, crying out as they are strangled by ivy. The thought amuses me and I smile. I start to admit to myself that I am imagining words and making meaning from sounds that have none.

There is nothing to see next door but weeds and wood chippings.

I walk back to the shed, and shut the door, slipping the padlock on. I wonder whether hearing voices, is a sign that gardening at St Osyth's Priory is getting too much for me.

"Let me out."

The voice makes me feel old, bewildered. I think perhaps the time has come to ask my daughter for help. But she is so unpredictable, one minute talking about meals-on-wheels and assisted living, the next fanning out retirement-home brochures on my coffee table.

Perhaps it is my hearing aid, the static sounding like sentences. I turn it off. The voice disappears along with the sparrow song and the beat of butterfly wings.

But it returns that night, in my dreams, relentless in its plea:

"Release me. Let me go."

And again in the morning when I turn my hearing aid back on.

"Let me go."

I think I am going mad. Not only that, when I look out of my kitchen window, I can see that someone has broken into my shed. The door swings on its hinges in the breeze. Should I ring the police? But what will I say? I don't want to become another old man on their time-wasting list. *Kids will be kids. Sounds to me like you need a doctor not a policeman.* In the end I take my own advice and ring my GP. Perhaps there is water in my ear canal making me unbalanced? There is always a rational explanation.

I pick up the receiver and start pressing the sequence of numbers. I have no trouble remembering them. I wait for the call to connect.

"GP surgery..." the receptionist answers.

Before I can answer her, sparks start flying out from the telephone receiver. There is a smell of burning plastic and thick grey smoke curls up from behind. I drop the handset onto the floor and step back, shocked. My right hand is red and a burning sensation travels up my arm. My flesh feels like it's melting.

"Ye burn in hell."

I stumble to the kitchen sink, turn the faucet on full, and let icy water run down my arm. In the back of my mind I can hear my daughter's voice admonishing me for not replacing *that old handset*. Eventually the stinging subsides, and I turn my hand over to inspect the damage, wondering if I will need to take myself to A&E. I cannot explain what I see. Apart from the usual liver spots, my skin is unmarked.

I walk back into the hall to check the telephone. It sits balanced on the Yellow Pages, like new. Like nothing has happened.

"Let me go."

The words slither into my eardrum.

I shake my head, trying to dislodge them and get them out.

"Dad. Dad. Are you there?"

"LEAVE ME ALONE," I shout.

"Dad I'm letting myself in. Father Bryan phoned…you didn't turn up at the Priory today…they were worried."

I hear the key turn in the lock and see a black patent shoe. For some reason I just stand there, dripping onto my hall carpet, frightened my daughter will think I can't manage anymore.

"Dad?" her voice is gentle, like her mother's used to be. "What's happened? Dad I'm worried about you."

I feel her take me through to the kitchen. I try to tell her about the voice and the telephone but I find each time I think about it, I feel the burning pain return. I see that I've left the tap on and the sink is overflowing. Water pools onto the lino.

"Dad, your skin feels very hot."

She sits me down at my table. I realise I haven't finished the crossword.

"Is it your heart?" she asks.

She is frightened I will die, or worse be a burden. I pick up the pencil and start to fill in the four blank squares. *BURN*. I wonder why I feel so angry, so disappointed. My daughter's voice drifts in and out, waves crashing against a sea wall.

"I'm going to ring an ambulance."

I feel a breeze against my back. My daughter must have opened the door. The warm air strokes me, urges me outside.

"Let me go."

I find I am stumbling over the threshold in my slippers, skidding on the damp grass. I cannot seem to move fast enough.

I barely notice my daughter at the bottom of the garden, shouting into her mobile phone, telling them it is an emergency, that she's got a bad reception.

"Release me."

I feel the voice coil around me and pull me faster towards the shed.

"Dad?"

I reach into the shed and pull the bottle from my coat pocket. I hold it in my hand. It's heavier than I remember, and filled with a green mist that beats against the glass, like a heart.

"Release me."

The words thud against my chest. The pressure makes me wheeze.

"Let me go. Let me go."

I feel myself falling. I know I should let go, toss the bottle into the garden next door, but instead I hang on tight as if it contains my last breath.

"Dad? DAD!"

My daughters panic seems remote. She speaks through fog.

"LET ME GO."

The voice in the bottle violates me, rapes my eardrums and my soul. I feel its anguish, its pain. I feel the injustice. It frightens me.

"LET ME GO."

I want it to stop.

I release the cork stopper.

I feel retribution push through my fingers. The swirling mist leaves its glass prison. I feel its desire for revenge as it evaporates.

Then I feel my daughter's cool hand on my forehead.

I am exhausted.

I do not know how long it takes before I hear the door creak and the grass whisper again.

I sit up.

"Dad?"

My daughter has her arm around my shoulders and is supporting me. She looks at me quizzically as I tip the bottle upside down: to make sure it has gone. A few dried herbs drop into my palm.

"I think gardening at the Priory might be getting too much for me," I say.

She helps me to stand, and makes me promise that I will make an appointment with my GP *to be on the safe side*. She does not mention 24 hour care or psychiatric intervention but instead leads me back to the house and makes me a cup of tea with a dash of brandy in it.

I do not tell her that later, when I hear St Osyth's Priory is on fire, it comes as no surprise.

Lynda Shepherd has been writing since school days, the bug bit and has never really left her. With encouragement from friends and family, she joined a local writers' circle almost a decade ago and started submitting her short stories to magazines and competitions. However this was not to be the source of her first publication, as following inspiration from a backstage tour she took of her local theatre 'The Queen's Theatre, Hornchurch' and the gleaned knowledge of their at that time forthcoming diamond anniversary Lynda researched and penned her first non-fiction article that was published by Essex Life in the September 2013 issue. Further joy was to follow, within a month she had heard that she had won third prize in a locally themed short story competition with the story we publish here 'A Little Light'.

She currently works full-time in an administrative role supporting her local government colleagues within children's social care. Lynda derives a great sense of warmth and pride from the small role she is able to play towards such important work. Lynda has a number of creative works in progress and hopes to be published widely in the future.

A LITTLE LIGHT

"*Ghosts!* You are not seriously telling me you believe in such hocus pocus are you?"

"It's tradition to leave a light on in the theatre, when the theatre's not in use."

"Superstition, there's a big difference and right now it's making a negative difference to our profits. You know the folding stuff that helps you get paid!" Richard mimed counting notes between thumb and forefinger.

"We're going!"

"Sam, Jonathan please stay. I'm sure Richard didn't mean to-."

"Don't tell me what I mean Sarah. Go, stay I don't really care but hear this, as of tonight the light goes off when that door closes."

Sarah stared at Sam, who exchanged looks with Jonathan.

"You're not serious?"

"Perfectly, I have to manage our finances and this superstition is something we can't afford."

"So you've not seen Banquo then?"

"Banquo, the bloke from M-," Sarah went to smack a hand across Richard's mouth, but she was too late, "Macbeth, what the-," Sam and Jonathan grabbed an arm each and propelled him out of the open fire exit onto the green towards Fairkytes. "Let go, for goodness sake, what do you think you are doing?"

They did not let go, but begun spinning him round; first one way, then the other and back around twice more.

"Now say the rhyme after me-."

"This is flipping ridiculous, I'm going back to my office. I have work to do, even if you don't!" Richard wheezed, as he stumbled back inside.

"Banquo stalks those very wings, if you don't believe me big man why don't you spend the night here tomorrow?"

"Monday," Sarah mouthed.

"I know it's another one of *those* traditions," Richard said directing a thumb at the departing actors.

"Don't you worry, when I prove you wrong, then it will be my way. No ifs, no buts, no blooming hocus pocus!"

"Tomorrow then."

"No problem John."

"Are you sure about this Rich?" Sarah said, packing up, the following night.

"You don't believe in ghosts?"

"Well personally I'm not sure, but I'm keeping an open mind."

"Its fine, see you in the morning."

Richard frowned, watching Sarah dodge the puddles as she hurried down the street.

Suddenly there was a loud rumble, then a flash of lightning that lit up the entire window. Richard shivered, he could have been out there too waiting for the 252. Doing the books had never been his favourite activity, but still he'd have a glass of whisky and he'd be fine.

Richard had put his pierce 'n' ping, plus a bottle of his favourite Fens whisky in the bar's fridge earlier. Theatre manager's perks and all that. Not bothering to turn on the lights just to further prove his point, he made his way to the bar and small adjoining kitchen. Sam was just silly. Didn't spend enough time in real world, that was his trouble.

When he opened the fridge door, he found the bulb had gone. *Typical*, now he would be forced to lift up Sarah's mysteriously silver foil wrapped packages until he found his dinner.

"Err..," something wet and squidgy had just landed with a horribly disconcerting splat on the tiled space in front of Richard's feet. Using the faint light from his mobile phone, he squinted to see what it was and then stared at the now spreading crimson tide. *Fake Blood.* Sam would've found that hilarious, it was an accident though, that's all.

Irritated, Richard flicked on the kitchen light. The strip lighting flickered half heartily into full brilliance, enabling him to find his *Chicken in Madeira Sauce with Crushed Potato for one* and his whisky.

Having cleared up the mess, whilst waiting for the ping, He plodded back towards his office via the auditorium. It was a strange thing, he loved this space. It was equally magical now in the shadowy darkness, the row upon row of seats awaiting the roar of another crowd. The pillars stood like centurions to either side of the parted sweep of curtain.

Richard brushed the back of his hand against the soft cherry velour pile of the seat to his left, before he set off up the steps and onto lacquered boards that squeaked beneath his plimsolls.

As he made the turn into the backstage area, his eyelids were suddenly forced down like a flesh coloured safety curtain as the white, hot spotlight hit him square on. His tray wobbled and he tightened his grip on its scalloped edges. *He must have knocked a switch.*

Just as he turned back and bent to operate the door handle to the office corridor with his elbow a voice boomed.

"As far, my lord, as will up the time 'twixt this and supper; go not my horse the better. I must become a borrower of the night. For a dark hour or twain."

"What the hell!"

Creamy white wine sauce, chicken pieces, shards of crystal splattered and ricocheted off his plimsolls. Richard's knees felt as though they might collapse from under him; there was no switch he could *have* accidentally knocked or flicked. *Not this time.*

He tried to think of a rational explanation for this almost ghostly happening. He didn't believe in the afterlife or all that hocus pocus as he had labelled it to his colleagues.

Had some teenagers sneaked in, looking for somewhere warm to drink cider and cause havoc? God, he sounded old.

Holding up his mobile, he searched the darkness for a lad with a dust sheet on his head. It wasn't bright enough, *where were the switches for main house lights?*

What was that? Footsteps, heavy booted footsteps. They were getting louder, nearer and louder still.

"Ay, my good lord. Our time does call."

Richard flattened himself to the wall, rooted to spot. That was no teenager, the voice was deep, confident and self-assured.

Get a grip, he told himself.

Stretching out a hand, he felt around for the switches. They must be here somewhere.

There it was again, footsteps. His heart pounded, finally a light flared out from the orchestra pit opening beneath the stage. Having inched forward, he jumped as he caught sight of a black velvet cape disappearing into the depths of the pit. *What now?*

Richard took a deep breath, pulling himself up to his full height. He was going down there and sorting this out once and for all. No-one or nothing was going to get the better of him. Decades old steps creaked and squeaked beneath him. *Ouch!* He rubbed his forehead, blinking as his eyes adjusted to the change in light as he stepped down from the final stair.

Over the other side of the pit he could hear a battle being fought with a door bolt. Now was his chance. He held his breath and tiptoed through the minuscule central aisle between the rusty music stands which scratched and rubbed at his flesh.

Just as the bolt slide across, he tripped and a heavy, well-thumbed score fell with a thwack to the floor. This side of the pit was in complete darkness, Richard had no choice but to leap forward making a grab for the cape. As he did so the door swung on its hinges, leaving him waist deep in a pool of jet black velvet. Standing up, he could hear the heavy footsteps retreating and a loud mirthless laugh slowly die away. Richard wasn't giving up, *where was this shadowy being going?*

He listened, listened harder. The foyer!

Richard hurried down the corridor, through the workshop and up a flight of draughty concrete steps, then another, round to the right and through into the foyer.

Everything seemed normal.

The foyer seemed huge in its deserted state, chairs stood in regimented polished rows ready for the next day. Leaflets fanned out in small piles on alternate tables.

"I will find you, you know. Give yourself up and it will look much better for you in the long run!"

"I will not, my lord!"

The laughter returned then, bubbling up, loud and wicked like the Macbeth witches preparing their cauldron.

Angry at fighting something or someone who clearly wasn't going to come out and face him, Richard marched towards where the sound of his torment seemed to be coming from. Ironically he was going full circle, heading towards his office.

He flung the door open, his breath ragged as he burst into the room. Seeing no-one he went over to his desk, but fell over his sleeping bag which stuck out just a few inches beneath. His chest went down on the swivel chair and he fell off chin first on to the threadbare carpet and hard man made floor.

Feeling winded, he struggled to sit himself up, leaning back against the cold metal filing cabinet. He looked out at the dark sky; he could see stars in more ways than one.

Hang on? What was that? He thought he could see a face, pale and sorrowful hovering by a door. Then suddenly an arm reached out and the image disappeared.

Richard felt like he was drunk yet he hadn't touched a drop; *surely it was just a bang on the head doing this to him. Wasn't it?* He wasn't sure now.

Maybe a little light wasn't such a bad thing after all.

Lloyd Bonson has been interested in cars since a young age and has spent all of his working life within the motor industry. From a production vehicle perspective he has been involved on many projects with Ford Motor Company, Jaguar Land Rover, Iveco Trucks, Aston Martin Lagonda and Volvo Cars.

In motor sport Lloyd was part of the Woodcock Brothers Racing team which won the UK Formula Saloons Championship in both 2000 and 2001 and the John Danby Racing Team which won the UK Sports2000 Championship in 2003.

For six years Lloyd was the motor racing correspondent for Phoenix FM radio in Essex, as well as hosting a variety of other shows including a motoring show called 'Overdrive'. Lloyd has also presented a variety of television programmes including the Ford Fiesta Championship, Porsche Club Championship, Mazda MX-5 Cup and a one off special for Castle Combe's 60th Anniversary.

His first book *One Hit Wonders: The Story of One Off Grand Prix Winners* has been critically received. Recently, he has been part of team of Archive Editors helping to transfer and maintain over 90 years of Motor Sport Magazine articles onto their website.

Away from cars, Lloyd loves rugby and is a proud supporter of London Irish; he is also a keen musician, singer, songwriter and amateur actor and is heavily involved with local dramatic and operatic societies in Essex, UK

AN ESSEX BOY RACER

The cars line up on the grid. It's a beautiful August afternoon in the Kent countryside as the International Formula 3000 Championship prepares to race around Brands Hatch. This is a re-start, an accident after the first start has caused the race to be stopped and reset.

At the front of the grid in Pole Position, sits a driver with dreams of making it into the glamorous world of Formula One. It would be a far cry from his upbringing around Romford. And it's a dream that was well within his reach; he'd already beaten over 100 drivers to win the Formula Ford Festival only three years before, had tested one of the most powerful Formula One cars of the day, and won on his debut in Formula 3000.

Good results in this race at Brands Hatch and the following weekend at Birmingham would be enough to convince the Benetton team to make him a Grand Prix driver the following year. The Pole Position time set in the first phase of qualifying was so large, that the driver didn't need to run in the second qualifying phase. Formula One was in touching distance.

It's just after 3.45pm on Sunday 21st August 1988. The flag has dropped and 21 cars scream up from the start line into Paddock Hill Bend. The re-start isn't good and our driver goes a little sideways and has slipped down to third before the cars make the first corner. As the field races up to the hairpin at Druids, there's a white car trying to get past, banging his wheels with our driver. The driver of the white car has been a hot-head all season, but as they come out of the hairpin the thoughts of the driver in yellow car are to attack the car in front, rather than defend the one behind.

Out of Surtees corner, the cars head out on the Grand Prix loop of the undulating Kent race track. This a long straight that rises, then dips under a spectator access bridge, through a section called Pilgrims Drop, before a fast 90 degree right hand bend called Hawthorns.

The white car goes to the left of the yellow one, as they reach the crest of the hill. They are racing at around 160 m.p.h. They make contact. Both cars spear off to the left of the circuit, as the run-off area narrows due to the bridge.

The yellow car smashes into the bridge head on. The white car hits the Armco barrier just in front of the bridge which pushes it back into the yellow car and forces them both onto the track into the path of other traffic.

They make contact with a third car – a turquoise coloured one – and now all three cars are heading towards the barrier on the other side of the track. Yellow coloured bodywork is flying through the air, this is part of the cars design, to dissipate energy from the accident away from the driver. The same is happening on the other two cars, as more bodywork and tyres go flying into the air causing danger for the cars which follow.

The white car is traveling sideways along the grass, when a tyre digs in and causes it to flip and cartwheel violently, it's driver is unconscious but alive. The turquoise car shoots across the track, the yellow car is spinning around and the other drivers try to avoid contact with these projectiles, but end up tripping over themselves.

In less than ten seconds, more than half the starting grid of cars are damaged beyond repair. What remains at the track could only be described as a plane crash scene, or the aftermath of a bomb explosion.

The driver of the yellow car feels he has stopped spinning. He opens his eyes. In front of him he can see there is a big hole in the front of the car. He can see his knees and nothing else. The track marshals rush to his aid and he shouts at them to knock him out, but they don't. He can't see the front of his car, nor his legs – although he suspects if the marshals find one, they'll find the other!

All his dreams are now dashed.

The marshals and medical team start to extract him from the car. It's a long process. One of the Japanese drivers comes over to make sure everything is ok, but our driver can see the expression on his face change as he looks down. His mind can't take anymore and he shuts down into unconsciousness.

The driver is removed from what remains of his yellow racing car and taken immediately to Saint Mary's Hospital in Sidcup, The management from his team and his own personal manager are also in attendance. The Doctor's fear they may have to amputate his left foot, the damage is so severe. They are persuaded to do anything possible to save his foot.

Many operations follow, there is uncertainty if the driver will ever walk again, let alone drive, or even race. What had promised to be a glittering career, was banished. How could he ever recover?

Sunday 26th March, 1989 and the sun is beating down in Rio de Janeiro, Brazil. It's the opening round of the Formula One Championship and Nigel Mansell has taken an impressive victory on his debut with Ferrari, after several seasons with the

Williams and Lotus teams.

There are other drivers making their debut Grand Prix that day. One of them is a driver who finishes in fourth. This is impressive for any debut Grand Prix driver, but it is even more impressive for this particular driver.

For this is the same driver who seven months previously, was driving a yellow car at Brands Hatch. It is the same driver who crashed into a bridge at around 160 m.p.h.. It is the same driver who Doctor's feared would need to have his left foot amputated.

This driver would go on to compete in 161 Grand Prix, winning three of them. He would also tackle the gruelling Le Mans 24 Hours race eight times, finishing on the podium in half of those races – including a victory.

The drivers name? Johnny Herbert.

Farleigh Hospice

Farleigh Hospice provides specialist hospice services to anyone over 18 from the mid Essex area living with cancer and other life-limiting illnesses. In addition to our care for patients we also provide a range of services for families and children. At any one time Farleigh is offering physical, emotional, social and spiritual support to around 1,400 people, free of charge.

A beacon of compassionate care in the mid Essex community

Farleigh Hospice had humble beginnings. After Audrey Appleton died of cancer in 1981 her friends recognised the need for hospice services in and around Chelmsford and launched an appeal. Over thirty years later, Farleigh Hospice continues to expand its services to provide high quality, specialised palliative care to the increasing number of people in need of hospice services.

Every day Farleigh Hospice needs more than £15,000 to provide doctors, nurses, bereavement counsellors and therapists. Whether a patient requires relief from pain, help to live independently, expert advice, specialist care in a comforting environment, or bereavement support for their family, Farleigh Hospice is there for them.

Support at times of greatest need.

The hospice building in Chelmsford has a 10 bed Inpatient Unit for respite and end of life care. Patients can make use of the full range of hospice services during their stay including treatments from complementary therapists and emotional and practical support from chaplains and social workers.

With many people with life limiting illnesses preferring to spend as long as possible in their own homes, the community nurses provide symptom control, specialist advice and support to enable this to happen. Last year Farleigh's team of community nurses made 3,267 home visits.

Farleigh Hospice also runs Day Services in Chelmsford and Maldon, where patients can benefit from a range of wellbeing and therapy activities. Other services include outpatient clinics, bereavement support and our mobile service, the Hospice Outreach Project (HOP) which visits high streets and public places to provide information, advice and support to the mid Essex community.

In 2015-16 Farleigh Hospice provided its services, totally free of charge, to 3,317 people and experienced a 17% increase in referrals. Purchases of this book will help Farleigh to care for the ever-growing number of people who need their support to live independently and with dignity.